Spiritual Awakenings

Volume 1

Cover by Daniel McCutcheon

For Cover Art Inquiries Contact:

mccutcheondan@gmail.com

1st Edition

Table of Contents

Introduction

Awakening to a spiritual path is an exploration of self-discovery, growth, and connection to something greater. It can be a transformative journey that reveals a deep connection to the world around us and the divine potential within. In this book, you'll read stories from our incredible authors about their Spiritual Awakening experiences. Throughout this book, we will explore the concepts of spiritual awakening, the ways to approach it, and how it can open up a new dimension of understanding and growth in our lives. These pages can help provide insight and guidance for your own spiritual journey.

We will often find that our values and priorities change when we awaken spiritually. We may become more interested in personal development and growth, being a service to others, and connecting with our Higher Selves. Our perceptions of the world may also change, and we may start to see the beauty and magic in everyday life. We may even find that we are drawn to new hobbies and activities that nourish our souls.

All of these changes can be scary and overwhelming, but they can also be intensely rewarding. As we open ourselves up to new spiritual realities, we often find that our lives become richer and more meaningful. We connect with our authentic selves, and we start to live more in alignment with our true purpose. We hope that it will inspire you to embark on your own journey of self-discovery and growth.

Kirsten Newman

Did you ever feel that this world simply wasn't meant for you? That you simply weren't meant for this world? This was my beginning, as it is for most lightworkers, shamans, priests/priestesses, channels, healers, witches, empaths, and energy sensitives. This sense of not belonging, of not being wanted, and of not wanting to be. This is a shadow that I knew for the first thirty years of my life, and it made my childhood incredibly difficult.

It's not that my parents weren't loving, they were and truly always have been. Yes, there were difficult times in our household, and yes there was, of course, trauma involved. I was expected to take on far too much emotional burden and maturity at far too young an age, as empaths often are, and was always the child who soothed the parents during the more challenging years. But I was loved, and I always knew I was loved. For that, I will forever be grateful.

The unconditional love from my parents wasn't enough for me at that time. It feels so wretched to own that truth because I am so incredibly aware of the number of people who would have given anything to have the love that I did. What I truly yearned for back then was the acceptance of my peers, and this was something that always felt beyond my reach.

I felt odd, as a child. Awkward. Unwanted. Unlovable. Rejected. Abandoned. Over-and-over again. This was the theme that seemed to play out for me in my childhood whenever I tried fitting in and making friends, and it wasn't made any easier by the fact that I found most children my age to be cruel, harsh, and near impossible to relate to. I simply didn't fit in, and I found school miserable and overwhelming. This is my main memory of childhood outside of my home.

At fourteen, my parents divorced. They were both at their unhappiest, both dealing with their own pain, and as I result, I felt they were completely incapable of seeing mine. I had slipped into a depression that made my entire body feel cold, dark, and heavy. I felt disgusting; like some strange creature from another planet that nobody could love, and my two parents, despite their unconditional love, just couldn't see it. I had worked too hard to be the emotionally mature one of the three children, the part of me that was always acknowledged and praised, and consequently, that had become a blanket of apathy that neatly concealed the true depths of my loneliness and heartache.

I faked a mysterious illness for the final year of school, unable to face another day of feeling unwanted, of being surrounded by people I didn't understand and who didn't understand me. Nobody questioned this illness, and I was allowed to play it out. I have since reflected on how truly depressed I must have felt during this time, that at just fifteen I was content to pretend to be unwell 24/7 for an entire year. To let each day slip by without my being any part of it. Perhaps that was my deepest fantasy back then... to simply fade away into nothingness.

I remember at this time seeing a Chinese herbalist for my acne and for the first time in a long time feeling seen, truly seen. This man would take time in our appointments. He would smile at me. He would ask me questions and listen patiently to my answers. He even offered to teach me how to drive off-road when I turned sixteen because I'd shared that it was something I was excited to do. He seemed to genuinely want to know more about me. I naively and gratefully drank it all in; this appreciation from an adult who didn't have to care for me or find me interesting to talk to, but who seemed to all the same.

As we got further into our appointments, he started asking me more personal questions that I trusted him enough to answer. Questions that an adult would instantly know were inappropriate, but that as a young teenager who was desperate for attention, simply felt comfortable answering. "Are you happy with the size of your breasts?" was the first inappropriate question I can remember now. As a flat-chested, late developer who felt like an unwanted child next to her taller, curvier peers, I shook my head. I wasn't happy with them. I wanted to look more mature; to have a body that I felt matched my emotional maturity. A body that I could look in the mirror and feel that, yes, it had finally grown into the young woman I felt I had mentally become many years prior.

"I can help you with this," he responded. He told me that regular massage would increase blood flow to the breast tissue and stimulate growth. I nodded without giving it a second thought. In truth, I was delighted to be in on this magical secret to changing my body, to changing ME. I thought, "Surely if my body looked more loveable then I would be more loveable also?" And so, each week, I would go to this man, and I would allow him to massage my chest.

Over time he started asking me more questions about other ailments I may have. Stomach issues? As an anxious teen, I nodded, and that was when the breast massages slowly extended into stomach massages, getting lower and lower each week until eventually, his fingers would curl around beneath my underwear.

The final day I saw him, without a single word to me, he pulled my trousers and underwear down fully so that he could look. That was when my body finally kicked in with a fear that was loud enough to cut through the numbness of my depression and let my brain know that something was seriously wrong and had been all along. Once again, I felt disgusting. I felt ashamed; so deeply ashamed. How could I have been so stupid? Was it my fault? After all, everything he had done up until that last day had been with my full consent...

I retreated further into myself, numbing with food and fantasies of characters in other worlds. I tried to tell my mum once about what had happened, but when the words got stuck in my throat and I simply couldn't speak them, she got angry and that further fed my shame. My dad, who had taken me to these appointments every single week for the best part of a year didn't question it when I suddenly stopped. Nothing was said, the shame was internalized, and nothing was done about it.

The next couple of years were uneventful for me, as you might expect for a teenager with no direction and no drive. I mostly engrossed myself in bringing my fantasies alive through my love of writing. Having found college another unbearable experience of not fitting in and having my strangeness repeatedly pointed out to me, I dropped out and settled for a weekend job at the library.

This was where I met him. The man who changed my entire world. The man who looked at me as a desirable woman, and not just a malleable girl. Or so I thought...

At eighteen, I found myself in a relationship with a man who was all the things I was not. Strong, confident, passionate, and sure of himself; the moment he saw me I felt my heart leap out of my numb body. To be seen, to be desired, to finally be the main character in a romance story instead of one of the clumsy, forgettable, side characters who simply fill the space in the background; I had truly yearned for nothing more. Once again, for the return of feeling seen and wanted, I sacrificed my intuitive knowing and power.

This man was not loving; he didn't know how. He had come from a childhood of abuse, abandonment, and grief, and knew darkness even more deeply than I did. But a strange thing happens when you finally feel seen by someone, even if they are your abuser. After so much time of feeling unseen, it's as though you believe to your very core that you might vanish from the world entirely if they were to ever leave you and stop seeing you. As though no pain they could inflict on you could be worse than that achingly deep pain of being invisible once again, of vanishing from life, of fading back into the abyss of your loneliness.

For seven years, even after being hospitalized for a time due to feeling suicidal, I was committed to him. Until one day, I simply stopped getting off the sofa. It had reached the point where he was so repulsed by me that I wasn't allowed in the bed anymore, and so the sofa was where I slept. It became where I slept all day as well as all night. He didn't comment, his friends would come and go, walking past me as I lay in my void. For the final few months of our relationship, this was my life; once again I was trying to fade away, to vanish from a world that I believed had never wanted me in it.

When I reached twenty-five, this man finally decided he didn't want me anymore, so I hastily packed my things and returned home to my dad, feeling a sense of relief, and looking forward to a new beginning that I wanted very much wanted to cling to. I weened myself gently off my antidepressants, for I did not need to be held in my emotional numbness any longer. With my older brother's help, I got a job. I started talking to people again, and this time, I didn't feel unwanted or judged by them. In fact, I even felt quite appreciated by some of them.

Just eighteen months after my breakup I met the kindest, gentlest, and most compassionate man. I wasn't looking for a relationship. I recognized that I was still a shell of a person and that I needed time to learn who I was; the very reason I had been mistreated in the past was that I had been so malleable. Yet, here was a man who fell in love with me anyway. It didn't matter how much ugliness I showed him, how much I tried to push him away or keep him firmly in the "friend zone", he could see in me something I couldn't, and he loved me for it.

We married two years later; soulmates, best friends, partners in crime forever. My husband, Tom, is everything my ex was not and is nothing that my ex was to me. There is no cruelty, no malice, no power trips, no mind games, no gaslighting, and no forcing: only kindness, love, and plenty of laughter and fun.

In 2017 our world changed forever when his dad unexpectedly passed away after a year of fighting and then beating his cancer. To say we were heartbroken would be the biggest understatement. There was no day in my life, not even the days of abuse, that could have been more painful than this day.

At the time, I was still very much living with my depression, but this plunged us both into the depths of darkness. Tom became suicidal and I became so very afraid that I would lose him. Together we somehow managed to keep each other going despite fighting our own inner demons. Perhaps it helped to have one another in the void. To not be completely alone.

People we had believed to be friends fell away, and bit by bit, I watched as the life I had worked so hard to build after all the years of sadness and abuse just crumbled. Gone. Over.

The cruelty of it stung within me. This sense that life simply didn't want me to succeed or be happy. That it was punishing me for even daring to believe that I might get to have the life I wanted. As I slipped deeper still into a depression that held me captive in my own bed, the greatest gift I've ever received was given to me... I was forced to listen to my body.

I was forced to listen to my feelings. To accept the darkness. To let it in fully and to surrender to it. What else could I do? The more I fought it, the harder my life had become. It seemed that life wanted me in this despair, so in a mixture of exhaustion, anger, and sheer resignation, I finally allowed it. I let all the grief, all the shame, all the anguish wash over me, wave after wave after wave. In this space, the most beautiful thing happened to me; I found a strange, albeit rather uncomfortable, sense of peace. The peace of self-acceptance. Of allowing myself to be everything I was in this present moment without any resistance or judgment. A peace I had never truly granted myself ever before.

Over time, I learned to build on this self-acceptance. I was entranced by how different it made me feel, how even the darkest of days could feel possible for me when I accepted myself fully. It was okay that I was gaining weight. It was okay that I wasn't eating properly. It was okay that I was in too much pain to work. It was okay that I needed time. All of it was okay.

The more I allowed myself to feel my body, to feel my emotions, the more that came up for me to heal. I started to acknowledge all the pain I had spent so long repressing and numbing myself to. I started to grieve all my past traumas so I could validate my experiences and hold myself in compassion. I sobbed as a tiny, frightened child would, and simultaneously held myself as a fierce and strong mother. It was here, in this dark time of deep transformation, that I unlocked one of my greatest gifts as a healer.

Adopting this duality is a huge way in which I serve my clientele to this day: holding others in their shadow and being their guide as they learn to lead themselves through. Holding the confidence and certainty for my clients to find their way through; until they can know it, feel it, and see it for themselves. For me, it is all about the body, all about what it stores, and what it is asking for us to release.

The day I learned about somatopsychic responses and how the body alters our well-being, and even our beliefs, something within me clicked and awakened that had never felt switched on before. After years of trying to change my life with my mindset and continuing to feel weighed down by my body, I finally understood the importance of letting my body lead the way in my healing journey and trusting that my mind would follow.

Our body stores so much. Not just our trauma, it stores our wisdom, and our soul truths as well. The more willing we become to listen to our bodies, to release that which is stagnant, to move, to awaken, to cleanse, to be in our darkness, yes, but to also be in our bliss, our pleasure, our desires, the more we can become the light that we were always here to be.

I truly believe our body is the portal to our greatness. I truly believe it took me so long to discover my own greatness because I had spent so many years numbing and detaching from my own body; in turn, rejecting my inner wisdom and intuitive knowing. I found myself grasping desperately for outward approval, understanding, and direction.

When we need to heal, it is our body that will tell us. When we need to change direction, it is our body that will tell us. When we need to rest, play, run away, or move forward, it is our body that will tell us. When we find ourselves stagnating in life, it is because we have allowed something to stagnate within. Learning to lead in my life through my body has made me feel more energized and alive than I ever believed was possible for me. It has shown me the gifts in every single moment, and it has connected me more deeply than ever to my soul purpose and to Source.

This is the medicine I am now passionate about sharing with others. The medicine of tuning into your own body, your own wisdom, your own purpose, and, in turn, finding yourself ready to share your own unique medicine with the collective too. For you to understand that you ARE meant for this world and that all your life experiences, the good, the bad, and the ugly, are meant for you. Not because you aren't loved by the Universe, not because you aren't supported, but because your greatest light of all must be found within the shadow, and the deeper you journey to find it the brighter the light you will discover.

Your brain doesn't need to figure it out. Your mind doesn't have to solve the problem, because your body already knows exactly where you need to be, what your next step is, and all that is in store for you when you follow your internal compass. What could possibly be more beautiful than that?

Crystal Wheeler

As a young girl, I was always so inquisitive and full of questions. When you saw me, I always had a smile on my face, however, deep down I was fighting something much deeper than the eyes could see. I grew up in two very different households. My mom and my dad divorced when I was only a year old, so my siblings and I lived with my mom for the majority of the year, and every summer break my dad would get my sister and me.

In my mom's household, we were taught what I like to call, "The Golden Rule" which is to always tell the truth, have a kind heart, and always lend a hand to those in need. The idea was that if you do those things and you will have an amazing afterlife. My dad's household was the total opposite. He was extremely religious and always brought us up with the notion that the church always came first. Every time those doors open, you had to be there. Not just any church either, it had to be a certain type of church, and if it wasn't "that" type of church, then it was wrong and frowned upon. So, every summer when we would go up there, we were expected to play the part of the sweet church girls. My sister and I were the girls who were baptized in name of Jesus, and we were expected to give our mind, body, and spirit, to the Lord.

When I was twelve years old, I remember asking my dad," Why don't we have music in our church?"

He replied, "Music doesn't belong in the church house." He also went on a huge, long tangent that churches with music were the house of the devil. That never sat well with me at all. But alas, I did what I was told, and I became the best daughter of the Lord. I read my bible every night and did exactly what I was supposed to do.

That was the year when he also started being harsh on my sister and me about our physical appearance. We were not allowed to eat after four in the afternoon. We had to look and present ourselves a certain way. That was the year that my eating disorder entered my life and my dark era began.

I began to question my whole life. There was a void in my heart that felt empty and unfulfilled. I felt that I was missing something that was supposed to make me feel whole and I began to search to find it. At fifteen years old, I came out of the closet as a lesbian. Later on at 28, I would find a man that I fell in love with, and from then on I began to identify as bisexual. It was a second coming-out experience.

Coming out at fifteen shocked my entire side of my dad's family. He immediately stopped talking to me, and this carried on for several years. My grandma expressed how disappointed she was in me. I was disowned and it broke my heart, but I couldn't help whom I loved and was attracted to. His side of the family and I eventually got on civil terms, but it took a long time.

That year was the year of my spiritual awakening. I stopped going to church and I went on a journey of self-discovery. I wanted to figure myself out. Who was I underneath it all? Who was Crystal without the facade of religion? You see, I was never comfortable being a religious conformist at all. I began reading about crystals and candles, manifesting, and magic, and I swear I never felt more at home. I felt peaceful and protected unlike I had ever felt. I simply just wanted to be.

My ears and eyes were completely open. I wasn't being judged anymore, I was simply me in the raw; I was finally home! I was marching to the beat of my own drum, and it felt right. I was boundless and carefree and that is what I always wanted. Was my story over? If you guessed no, you would be correct. Struggling with my eating disorder never went away. I just put my focus on other things for a while, even though I stopped hiding the fact that I had feelings for the same sex.

I hid my hatred and obsession with food. I started restricting my food and became bulimic. I hated my body and would speak nothing but self-body negativity. You wouldn't ever catch me getting ready in front of the mirror, after all, the mirror and I were sworn enemies. I became obsessed with my scale and weighing myself fifty times a day became my normal. It shouldn't have been but that was my reality. I developed a bad relationship with food and eating food started feeling more like a chore than a pleasant experience. It invaded my mind. I know it sounds silly, but anyone who struggles or has struggled with an eating disorder knows where I am coming from.

I needed to get it under control, and fast. I hated the way clothes fit me; I hated the way food made me feel super uncomfortable. So, I started my self-confidence journey. I started my path to heal myself on the inside and the outside. This journey is still happening at this very moment. It's something I'm always going to fight, but healing is not easy, nor is it supposed to be, and it has no end.

You are meant to love yourself and the skin that you are in. You should love every part of your body, even those that you consider flaws. You deserve self-love! Self-love is pure magic and there is nothing like it. So, while I am on my journey of healing my eating disorder and becoming the best version of myself, I'm also digging deep into my spirituality.

I decided to get out of my comfort zone and started my leggings business called LegsForDaze. I am on a mission to help women across the globe find themselves and love themselves. My goal is to make them feel confident, strong, and empowered when they put on a pair of my leggings. I want them to look in the mirror and think, "Damn, I look good." I want to inspire them to give a fuck about themselves. To put self-care first. I want to show them that no matter what your size is, you are beautiful in every way, shape, and form. My leggings will make a big impact!

I want my leggings to help them look in the mirror with positive intentions. If you don't think you are the hottest thing since the sun, then what are you doing? Wear that outfit you are putting off. You deserve to walk around feeling like your best self. You deserve to walk around feeling like you are on top of the world and thriving. Your body is your temple and I want you to cherish it. That is exactly what my mission is with my company.

All women across the world should love their mind, their body, and their spirit. My company may be starting off tiny, but it will grow big and mighty. The foundation was built on many tears, but also, inner strength, and passion as deep as the ocean. No matter what path you are on, I can promise you this: the moment you have your spiritual awakening is the moment you start to find yourself. That's when your real journey starts!

The best advice I can give you is to take your time. Go through your experience, and no matter what, never give up or let anything dull that shine in your soul. You are powerful! You are warmth and light, and you will always end up exactly where you need to be. Just trust the whole process, not just half of it. My name is Crystal, and I am in it for the long haul. My journey is not over yet... it's just beginning.

Alea Marie Quiles

Intuition Activated

"Did you hear that?" I said to my older sister. She looked at me with wide eyes and fright in her brows. "Yeah, it sounds like running water," she said. Trembling, we walked together to the bathroom faucet. The tap was on, but no one was near the bathroom and no one else was in the house. "How?" I questioned her.

This is the question that has been in the back of my mind since I was a child. We grew up in a haunted house and I was a sensitive child. This was one of many instances where the unexplained paranormal aspects of life were presented in mysterious ways and made me question reality as well as the nature of the universe.

There had been an old couple who'd passed away in the house, and they insisted on listening to jazz and swing music with the upstairs radio while creaking the floorboards when I was home alone. They would turn faucets on and off, walk up and down the hall, make shadows, and whisper in the laundry room. I would get prickles on the back of my neck. I was scared but I felt that these spirits weren't malevolent.

However, I had a spirit that followed me since I was a small child. One day, he appeared without warning and opened the fridge, across from where I was sitting. He slammed it shut to get my attention. SLAM! It jolted me from my seat and sent me into a panic. I was terrified and home alone. I didn't grow up religious, but you better believe that was the day that I learned to pray and denounced all my gifts, talents, and my ability to see the world beyond.

After that, I never saw anything again. What I didn't expect was the void it would cause within my soul. This would eventually send me on a journey towards a spiritual awakening, not long after my Saturn Return, in my 30s.

Years passed and I went about a somewhat normal life growing up in Alaska. In my late teens, I found a good paying job in Seattle. Yet, a decade in personal banking left me broken and dispirited. I suffered a mental breakdown, most likely caused by PPD after giving birth to my first-born son.

I quit my job, college, and stayed home to be with my toddler. It was in the wake of this chaos that I began my journey of Shadow Work, inner work, diving into my creativity, and soap making. Giving the sadness, grief, and pain a place to reside outside my body came as an expression in the form of soap, usable art. Cleaning and ridding my physical body of the things that no longer served my greater good. Cleansing my aura and becoming a new me. Growing up spiritual with the belief of something beyond, but not practicing and shunning my gifts, left a hole inside my heart that I feared would leave me shattered and empty.

When I started to lean into my creativity and my intuition, I allowed myself to experience magic as well as wonder again; I saw parts of myself come alive and had a renewed sense of self. I was coming home to myself... it was a remembrance of love.

I began to remember the wonderment of my childhood. How I felt when I was inside the spiritual and curio shops, working with herbs and natural ingredients, was pure excitement; it gave me an uplifting sense of joy. Purpose began to awaken within the chambers of my heart. It was very much a homecoming to my soul's truth. I remember consuming every bit of material I could get my hands on about spiritual awakening. I poured over countless blogs, books, courses, and content that helped me make sense of the experiences and sensations I was feeling.

"Am I going crazy?" I thought to myself.

A spiritual awakening is not what you would picture it to be. The clouds do not part, nor do angels descend from the sky with heavenly voices and harps. A spiritual awakening is an event that makes you question absolutely everything:

Who are you?

What are you doing on this planet?

How did you get here?

What is your purpose?

Are you happy?

Do you love yourself?

Do you like the company you keep?"

Why do you have so many material possessions?

Are you following your passions, likes, and joy?

What happens when we pass on?

More often than not, these questions will lead you on a journey of the Shadow Path a.k.a. deep self-reflection and/or The Dark Night of The Soul. You may feel a plethora of emotions, from euphoria to deep sadness and pain from your choices and past mistakes. But do not fear it, do not give the emotions meaning. Allow them to move through you and experience them as they are. Do not store them in your body. Wait for the next step in the path to present itself as it's guided by the light of your intuition.

It's my firm belief that many people who are artistic, creative, writers, poets, neurodivergent, musicians, creators, crafters, builders, and makers, have been visited by the great muse. They have seen things that can not be easily explained. They have experienced something out of the ordinary and that's considered unusual. They have had visions, realizations, epiphanies, or have had an experience that left them breathless, connecting them to something "greater," something "beyond" this collective reality.

Yet not all spiritual awakenings have to do with mediumship, seeing the dead, talking to ghosts, or tragic accidents. Sometimes it just happens. Sometimes it is revealed through reflection, questions, and inner exploration.

I have a feeling that if you are reading this book, you can relate. You have a pull. There is something that is leading you and guiding you. You may have had a spiritual awakening already, or you are increasingly interested in learning about yourself in a new way, understanding your gifts, talents, passions, or purpose, and getting answers for the unknown.

At the beginning of my awakening, I was trying all sorts of new stuff, (from decluttering my space to meditation) to experiencing things I had never experienced. One day, I asked my spouse to meditate with me through eye gazing. Eye gazing is a form of meditation where you can look into your own eyes in a mirror, or you can gaze into the eyes of another person. This is a powerful technique to help experience a merging into oneness. When we sat down to do the exercise, I was nervous to tell you the truth, but I decided to trust the process and my partner.

After about ten minutes of eye-gazing meditation, it was as if the whole room had vanished, and I could only see a blurry image of my partner surrounded by a bright yellowish-orange silhouette. I could feel and see his energy. This helped me remember that ever since I was a child, I could see auras. "How cool!" I thought to myself. Then I had an "ah-ha" moment, where I intuitively had a knowing that this color must correlate to the Chakra system, which I had heard of, but didn't know anything about. I remember thinking, "This color has to relate to the Sacral Chakra", the pleasure center, where creative energy is stored. This made a lot of sense, because let me tell you, the tension in this room after eye gazing was thick enough to cut with a knife, if you know what I mean.

The next day, I did some research to validate what I had experienced, and sure enough, the Sacral Chakra resonates to the color orange.

As you can see, the lesson that helped me grow into the person I am now was learning to trust my intuition above all else. Your intuition is the tether that connects you to the universe. It is the piece of you that is left over from the creator. It is a spark in the deep vastness of space, time, and your soul. Your intuition is the greatest muscle you have, and it is worth strengthening.

I can't count how many times I should've listened to my intuition throughout my life and didn't. Learning to trust the pull and that inner calling is one of the hardest lessons and obstacles to overcome for all of us. Our society has all but snuffed out our intuitive side in favor of logic and reason. When our intuition speaks to us, most of us start to perceive it as a very quiet sense. Sometimes it's so subtle that it is easily dismissed and brushed off. Other times, our intuition can be so loud that it is hard to ignore, like in times of crisis.

My intuitive prowess has been harnessed and developed through rigorous practice, and yet I don't always get it right either. My intuition comes hard and fast and most times I don't have time to react because I'm still processing. Your intuition may have a slow build, or you might experience it as something completely different. Learning about your unique way of tuning into the universe around you is what matters.

Let me illustrate this by telling you a story about a time when I heard my inner voice. It was about nine years ago, way before my awakening. Although I was spiritual by nature, I hadn't really found myself within that community yet. I was standing outside, under this beautiful birch tree, I loved its bark, and was admiring its beauty. I was calm, at peace, and open to receiving. I closed my eyes as I touched its trunk, and that's when I heard it say, "Bethala." What the heck just happened?! This tree just talked to me! And it gave me its name?! I was so confused and shrugged it off to my imagination but never forgot the experience.

Some years later, during my awakening, I was reminded of this occurrence, so I decided to look up the meaning of the name Bethala; if there even was one. On a Google search, I found the name and the meaning. The meaning for Bethala is "Tree." I was SHOCKED. I had never in my life heard this name before and here it was in black and white with a meaning that was congruent to the experience.

Several years after that, I started my Druid Apprenticeship. We learned the sacred Ogham, the different trees for the year corresponding to the Celtic Tree Calendar, and the symbolism as well as the healing and metaphysical meaning of each tree. The first tree we were introduced to was Birch. The Ogham for Birch is... Beth.

If I did not have the courage to listen to my heart and follow my intuition, I would not have had my spiritual business, Alchemy with Alea, and the business I have now, Becoming Clutterless. Nor would I have become a multi-published published author, which has been a literal dream come true. As a Reiki Master Teacher, I have gone on to connect clients with their Elemental Guides and have predicted things like career changes, pregnancies, and opportunities. By listening to the whisper of the universe, lit my soul on fire and led me down a path that not many have the courage to travel. It is windy, and it is sometimes dark, but it is also a place that leads you straight into your soul. You know those pieces of yourself that feel missing, the ache at your core, the questions of who you really are, the wonder of life, and the craving for true freedom; it all starts with curiosity and a calling for your creativity.

A spiritual awakening usually starts with a hunger for more. A curiosity about what it means to be alive. A quest for meaning. A journey for fulfillment. When you feel those things, follow the energy of your joy, your wonder, and your passion, just watch for synchronicities, miracles, or signs that will point you to the next opportunity.

As for me, the light and joy that is leading my life right now, is thinking about the good I can do with writing, decluttering, organizing, and intuitive home interiors. The impact that I can create and the help I can provide. I've lived a good and curious life where I have gained so much knowledge and wisdom. I plan on sharing my lessons through books, articles, group sessions, in-home and online support, and wherever else the wind carries me.

I always trust that everything happens for a reason, that the Universe, God, Source, Goddess, Creator, Earth Mother, or however you wish to name your higher power, is always guiding, providing, and supporting.

It is my hope that by the end of this book, you have enough evidence to feel and trust your center. It helps to build an unshakable faith within you as well.

I cannot stress enough that learning how to tap into your intuition is one of the most invaluable skills and gifts that you can give yourself. Your intuition will lead you to places you never even knew were possible, and the more you listen and follow it, the more magical it becomes. You see, intuition is as much a muscle as your heart and brain. It is your belief (in anything) that makes your reality. Your intuition is sacred. Do you know what sacred means? It means "to sacrifice."

Sometimes your intuition will make you do things your ego didn't want, but your spiritual self knows it's the right thing to do. It helps make hard decisions that sometimes bring you to your knees. Sometimes it will pull you out of your comfort zone so far, you won't even recognize yourself. The common thread? It ALL happens for a reason. Some things need to be sacrificed in order for new and bountiful doors to open. It may be hard to see the good of it when you are going through it, but the joy on the other side will be worth every challenging moment.

To practice strengthening your intuition, which I cover in greater detail in my book Activating Your Inner Alchemist, all you need to do is have patience and belief. The belief can be in yourself, in a higher power, in possibility, or whatever feels good to you. Quiet your mind with a few cleansing breaths, close your eyes, and practice feeling what your intuition feels like to you. Remember a time when you listened to your intuition, like when you were driving in a neighborhood and found your dream house or stopping by a thrift store on a whim and finding your perfect wedding dress, or having a hunch that you lost your jewelry in the garden, and finding it exactly where you thought it might be. As you go through this process ask yourself:

Where in your body do you feel this nudge?

This hunch? This calling to act?

How does it feel?

Are you light and airy? Joyful? Do you have a sensation of some kind?

Write it down in your journal and practice listening to and following this energy. This is also where you may become aware of your clair senses a.k.a. clear senses (clairvoyance, clairaudience, clairsentience, clairalience, clairgustance, and claircognizance).

If you are a person who struggles to determine if it's intuition or fear that you're feeling, then you're in the right place. This is very common, and you are not alone. You have every right to start slow and gentle when it comes to understanding your intuition, there are no quantum leaps necessary. To start slow and gentle, practice with your intuition on a daily basis with trivial things. For example, ask your intuition what you are craving to eat and nourish your body with. Hold pantry items, fruits, veggies, etc. in your hands and see what makes your heart light up. Then eat it, provided that it is something you know you can eat raw, cooked, prepared, etc. Be mindful of how your heart, mind, spirit, and body respond to this intuitive eating practice.

You can try this practice with so many other things as well i.e., clothes, kids, family pets, plants, spouses, friends, traffic lights, parking spots, events, trends, news, etc. Try intuitively picking your outfit for the day. Practice intuition with your kids. Ask them to choose a color and then you tell them which one you think they are thinking of. Pick up on the energy of your pets. Are they hungry? Bored? Want love or a walk?

Plants are such a fun way to practice your intuition too. Plants need soil, sunlight, water, and care just like anything else. Try picking up on the energy of your plants by standing near them, holding their pot, or touching their leaves gently if they're safe to touch, and see what comes through. Ask them in your mind, "What do you need today?" "Do you like this spot?" "Where would you like to move to?" and just wait for the answers!

At this point of self-exploration, the worst thing you can do is to question yourself. After all, these are fun practices, and nothing serious hangs in the balance if you just happen to get it wrong. This is where trust, faith, and belief come in. You must trust that inner voice, that feeling, that knowing, that you are connected to something unseen and it's a powerful force for good.

I love my plants dearly, as if they were my children. I cannot count how many times I've saved a plant from root rot, too much shade, too much sun, etc. Just recently, I noticed my Aloe was looking a little, unlively. So, I asked her what she needed. When I listened, she sprouted almost a dozen new babies!

The adventure of following your intuition isn't always for a grand creation, invention, or novel book idea. Sometimes it sheds light on the most precious things in your life. Creating new perspectives for gratitude and joy.

All in all, over the years I have predicted (and not just me!) the boom of YouTube make-up stars, the failure of Blockbuster, the rise of Netflix, the rise of Amazon, van life, as well as the development of our very own city that would increase the price of our home more than double, as well as many, many more turns of events and confirmations for clients. It all came about from my journey inward and the development of, and trust in, my intuition.

There is no better day than the present because it's a gift. Don't be like me and spend years denying your talents. Trust your intuition and the will of the divine. Develop your senses with the help of the Universe. Your inner knowing is waiting to be trusted and the day to be seized. Today can be the start of your creative activation; it's just one decision away.

Sarah Lines

The Dark Night Catalyst

I felt like an empty vessel. Soulless. No one and nothing could fill the void I'd been carrying with me my whole life. No amount of drugs, alcohol, or sex could fill my need to feel something different; anything different from the pain and dread that followed me day-in-and-day-out.

Even as a little girl, I'd always felt so deeply alone. I felt so different from everyone else, like I was an alien or something. Little did I know back then, how true this internal inkling actually was!

I was such a sensitive soul. So open and loving with beautiful gifts to carry. But these gifts I had, often felt like a curse: feeling the pain of others, feeling the collective suffering of humanity, it was too much to bare most of the time. I didn't know these feelings weren't mine, so I felt something was very wrong with me. I believed I was just destined for a life of sadness, anxiety, depression, and being deeply unfulfilled.

The pain of my childhood and the suffering I experienced throughout my adolescence was just the beginning. I turned to substances and sex to make me feel better, but I could never get enough. I kept searching for the next man to save me from my torturous existence, but of course, he never came.

After enduring toxic relationship after toxic relationship, I developed a strong sense of worthlessness. I believed I was unlovable and that I would never know true happiness or love; I convinced myself that that stuff was just in the movies. So, I kept using drugs, kept searching for my miracle man, and feeling like a useless human being.

I had 3 beautiful children by the age of 25. Even though from my earliest memories, all I had wanted was to be a mum, I ruined it. I was so spiritually sick I couldn't drag myself up to the level I needed to be at for my children to give them a good life. The life they deserved. Instead, they watched me struggle with myself, drink, do drugs, and have different men over all the time. I was so torn between the pain I was feeling and the love I had for my children... but I didn't know how to get better.

I kept drinking, using drugs, and sleeping with random men, because these were the only tools that I had at the time to put a pause on my inner turmoil. Even if it was only ever temporary. I was enduring a total dark night of the soul, and I didn't know it.

Just when I thought my life couldn't get worse, I met the boyfriend that would change it all. Together, we started injecting meth, but our cravings for the drug grew hungrier and hungrier and soon we turned to crime.

I fought it for a while. When he first came to me with the idea of selling my underwear on Craigslist, I said, "No!" He came to me again and again with the idea and I continually said, "No." However, after some time, when we were both chronic drug addicts, I finally caved in and said, "OK." I felt absolutely disgusting just even thinking about doing it, but it quickly became our new normal: driving to meet men all over Melbourne, to sell them my underwear, to support our habit. This escalated into meeting up with men for sex, but then we would take their money and drive away.

I'll never forget the time we were meeting up with a man, a biker, and even though I was drug affected, I had a really bad feeling. I told my boyfriend that this was not a good idea, but he insisted we follow through. I walked up to the man's black RAV4 and told him my usual line, "I gotta take the money to my driver and grab my bag." As soon as he realized that I was not coming back, all hell broke loose. He tried to smash his way into the car, and when we took off, he was immediately chasing us in his car. He had a gun pointed at our car and we tried everything to get away. We were speeding up going down the wrong side of the freeway to get free of this man, who was simultaneously calling me at and telling me to, "Get my pussy back now or give him the money back."

We drove to the closest police station and told them everything. I was shaking in my boots and vowed never to allow myself to be put in this situation ever again. Even though every cell in my body, and my entire being, was screaming at me to leave my boyfriend and go home, I didn't. Instead, we became so-called vigilantes and would blackmail pedophiles that thought they were coming to have sex with a 15-year-old girl. Instead, they would be met by my boyfriend. Where they would be given an ultimatum: to give us money or he would turn them in.

This was a dark world I never even knew existed. We traveled interstate to escape the dangers we had created for ourselves, being watched by certain dangerous people. I knew my life was in danger. After Christmas day in 2013, with dinner still on the table, and the Xmas tree still up, we left everything behind. I would never see my home or belongings again.

We spent months on the road, living in the car, using drugs, and stealing. This didn't last long; in April 2014 we were both arrested for extortion. "Thank

God," I thought, as a part of me was relieved. I kept thinking, "It's finally over." Unfortunately, this story wasn't quite over yet. Every time I thought I'd reached my lowest point, I quickly discovered I could go lower.

I spent 2-weeks in maximum prison while I waited for bail. I promised myself I'd never use drugs again. My boyfriend flew to Sydney to meet me when I was released on bail, and we were shooting up drugs almost immediately. We had a fight and he hit me for what felt like the millionth time, and for some reason at that moment, I finally knew that he would never change. Looking back now, I can't help but think, "Ummmmm-der!" but living through it is always different.

I rang my mum in Melbourne, sobbing my heart out, telling her I'd finally had enough. My sister came to pick me up on the northern beaches of Sydney where we had ended up, and she took me back to her place. Even with the best of intentions, my drive to end my pain was greater than my desire to get better. For 6 months I felt like a gypsy, hanging out with other drug addicts, and using. I met a really good-looking guy through these circles of people, and he took me in for a little while. We shot up together on our first date; looking back now, I can see this relationship was destined for failure. Again, der! I was blind to how sick I really was.

It wasn't until I found myself in psychosis, and thought everyone wanted to kill me, that I knew it was over for me for good. I could feel it in my bones that I was going to die from this addiction. I was working as a casual on a chook farm and I was horrified that the shed of 2,000 chooks were all screaming my name. "I can't do this anymore," my soul needed me to make changes.

I desperately wanted my children back. I felt like there was nothing more left for me to keep on living, my children were the only reason why I was still alive. It was a cloudy day in Windsor New South Wales (NSW), I had no one left in my life, no one that would pick up the phone when I called, not even the drug addicts I had been hanging with.

I walked into St. Vincent De Paul with an appointment for food vouchers with an elderly couple and I completely broke down. I knew I couldn't continue living how I was, but I had no idea what I needed to do. So, for some reason, I opened up and bared my heart to these people. I had nothing left to lose. I told them I needed help. The elderly man put his hand on my shoulder, looked me in the eyes, and told me it would be OK. I wondered how he could touch me let alone look at me, "If only he knew the things that I've done..."

This man was my Earth Angel. He and his wife helped me get into a private detox facility, and then after, to a long-term rehab center 8 hours away. He gave me his personal suitcases and helped me get warm clothes. The long-term rehab facility I was booked into was in the table mountains of NSW which gets very cold in Winter.

The last day I ever saw them, they dropped me off at the train station, and he gave me a bracelet. It was a Ste. Christopher pendant tied to a blue rope. As he tied this around my wrist, he told me how this too was gifted to him over 40 years earlier when he first came into recovery. It then all made sense to me why they were so helpful, and I'll never ever forget them, they gave me a second chance at life.

On the train, I took my SIM card out of my phone and changed my number. I was leaving my old life behind and was truly ready to do whatever it was going to take to change my life. I felt completely guided by unseen forces from this moment onwards.

It was a rocky first year in recovery, leaving my old life behind, but I felt driven by a strength I'd never known before, to keep doing the next right thing. I started meditating and handing my will and my life over to my higher power every single day. I couldn't believe I was clean and staying clean. Not only that, but I was also getting the mental health support I'd needed for a very long time.

I made friends with other recovering addicts and started laughing again. I started to believe there could be a light at the end of the tunnel. Within 12 months of getting clean, I got my little boy back. I was working as a support worker and felt a deep connection to spirit. It was like I was starting to wake up from a long dream. Everything up until this point in my life felt like a fog, but now I was feeling truly alive.

Then, I lost my nan, a young girl who was my friend's daughter, and I had a miscarriage all within 6-months of each other; this ignited something inside of me to start searching for answers to questions I'd never really asked before. I had to know more about our souls. I went deep into the rabbit hole of spirituality and never came back out!

I see this awakening as my second life in this life; the good, best life. I became a Reiki Master in 2016 and through that experience, I felt like I'd discovered true magic for the first time. Reiki opened me up in so many ways. It was like the gateway to everything. I started feeling connected with my soul, feeling the intuitive nudges guiding me to the next step, and then the next after that.

During this time, I had gone through all the motions to get my midwifery registration back, after losing it through addiction. I was so proud of myself, but I had this gnawing feeling that there was something else I had to do with my life. For some illogical reason, I followed that feeling instead of logic. It was difficult because everyone was so proud of me for getting my registration back, and midwifery is an honorable career. I had to follow my gut, I knew it wouldn't go away, and I was done with living a half-life.

I opened a healing room and got clients here and there, but I knew I had to go deeper and bigger. I had no idea why or how, but I trusted that it was my path. I decided to take my business online and that's when I realized I had so many internal mental blocks! Phew, did I ever have blocks... I had money blocks, invisibility blocks; seriously just about every block to being seen, heard, sharing my gifts, being intuitive, and being compensated financially for my services.

I hired business coaches, healers, and mentors to guide me through my first couple of years. It felt like every time I cleared another block, my soul got to shine brighter. I now get to help other women do the same, and I'm truly blessed to do so. I just love everything spiritual! I feel at home in this energy.

My gifts have re-awakened through this process. I know when someone is lying to me, I know if someone has good intentions or not, I know the highest potential of my clients, I see the higher perspective in all situations, I feel individual and collective energy, and I talk to my angels, guides, star family, and other beings every day. I feel truly limitless living life with this awareness, which is why I want this experience to be available to others! I truly believe when you listen to your soul that you are guided to your highest expression of self.

I want everyone to know that they aren't alone on this planet. We have so many beautiful benevolent beings supporting and loving us. I know this planet can feel dense, scary, lonely, and struggle-sum at times, but when you realize it's all an illusion and that you can choose to wake up from the dream, then absolute miracles can and do happen.

I know now that my soul was contracted to come to Earth to observe the struggles and trauma that I experienced so that I could learn from them and overcome them. I also know my mission here is not complete, that there is something even bigger I have to do on the planet, and I trust that every day I serve my purpose and will be led to the next step. I am studying to become a doctor of metaphysical sciences and I can't wait to see where this path leads me. Although I already feel truly blessed, that I live my life on purpose and with happiness, I know the best is yet to come as I help usher other souls into New Earth.

Taylor LaShay

SMACK

It's the gut-wrenching sound that fills the air as the bible my father was holding hits my mother's face. That was the day my world and all I knew about the spiritual world went up in flames. That day I started to question everything I was brought up to believe in. Too bad at the time I couldn't see it as the awakening it really was. That day, the universe spoke to me straight up, "Fuck everything you thought you knew!" Despite the feeling of an ending, that day ended up being the beginning of a journey to finding my faith, soul, and self.

I remember being so shaken because the altercation I witnessed really went against all I had learned up to that point. It felt like a holy war in my head and my heart. Cosmically though, I know now that at that moment I was being spiritually awakened to the fact that there is so much more, that it was up to me to search for it and make sense of my reality.

Soon after that incident, my mother and father separated and for a while, religion and spirituality ceased to be mentioned, we stopped going to church, and life went on. At least, it went on until it all came to a mind-bending halt when I found a book in the library with bright pink words that said, "Marked." I was drawn to this book on a level I couldn't understand at the time. I got started reading immediately and that was the day I marked myself for a reality crashing shift.

This entire book was all about a teenage girl discovering her natural born gifts after they got activated while still part of her "normal" life. She ended up being met by someone who took her to a school for the gifted that was full of students, all of whom had these natural gifts that connected them to all the elements of the world. I was not only marked as of the end of chapter one; I was also completely hooked and ended up spending a week binging all the books in the series, eating several bags of sunflower seeds for meals, because I was HOOKED.

I learned that the authors of the book are pagans, so I began researching paganism. That's when I learned all about how interconnected I, as a human, am to all the natural elements of the earth. This was rooted in the idea that I could use these elements like magic... so, I did. I started playing around with the way I viewed the world and my relationship with it, that is until my mother found out that I told our roommate's daughter I was pagan... I got in trouble and was told I was too young to understand anything about, "all that stuff."

So, I dropped it because a trusted source told me it was not real. The magic was gone as quickly as it came, this time though, it stayed away for a lot longer.

Then, a few years later, my mom and I had to move back in with family on our family farmland due to life circumstances and poor choices. That's when weird stuff started happening. One night, my little brother was crying in his crib in the room we shared, and my mom didn't get up. I wondered why she hadn't come to check, that's when I got up to try and find out what was going on, and then I realized I couldn't move at all. I could see a dark figure over my brother's crib but all I could do was look and cry from fear.

The next day, I decided to talk to my mom about what I saw, and she told me that she saw it too. That was the day my mother opened up to me about the religious and spiritual oppression she had faced and decided that it was unfair to put me through that any longer. So, we talked about years of interactions with spirits, and I even got my mom to read the marked series! I felt free again, at least in my ability to continue learning more about spirituality and religion.

My learning journey came to a halt when after years of family drama, trauma, drug abuse, and personal hardship, I just stopped learning as I was busy simply trying to survive. I moved away from home at seventeen with nowhere to go, and nothing but a laundry basket of my things. The only thought on my mind was about getting by and not ever having to go back home. Time went on, things kept shifting and changing in my life as I couch-surfed while working my shitty fast-food job and trying my best to get my damned diploma. I was living a very surface-level life, mostly focused on survival, and always left with a feeling of lack from my life, my relationships, my jobs, and my friendships. It was like, "What's even the purpose?"

Well, the answer to that lingering question soon found me. The real awakening happened a few years later. I ended up graduating and kept working my fast-food job. There was one day I had gone through one of the worst nights I had ever experienced at this job, and I was on the verge of giving up. Then a regular customer came up and said to me, "I don't know how you deal with this stuff, but you're always happy and you show up controlled, so I have an opportunity for you." That day, I got offered a chance to come interview for a management position for a retail store selling one of my favorite material items... SHOES! I thanked him several times over and went to the interview. The interview went great, and I got the position, but had to work at a different store than the one he did. At first, I was worried and had no idea what to expect.

The store I ended up going to work at had a store manager with a personality I had not yet come across. The store manager, Emma, changed my life by opening my mind to what truly could be a reality for me, no matter what had happened on my path. It all started with her training me and the statement, "I need to know you can manage yourself and the store when I am not around." I had no idea how the hell I was going do that, but something in me was just fully ready for what was to come. What unfolded over the course of that year was a beautiful friendship that taught me it's okay to question everything, especially my existence! What also came was the realization that if I wanted a better life, I had to get to know myself and re-work the negativity in myself.

On top of this new job, position, and a new caliber of human in my life I was experiencing; I also had just gotten into a relationship after being single, by choice due to trauma, for about a year. Around the same time, Emma told me, "I really enjoy being around you as well as talking with you, and I say this with love, but you can be really negative sometimes."

Then, my partner and I got into an argument that I initiated, and I left the house, toxically wanting to be chased. That's when I called him and he said, "Taylor, I want you around, I don't need you around." Two statements that let me know I didn't really know who I was or what I stood for. I saw that I was reacting and still living from an energetic space of hurt, anger, and lack mindset. Great realization. Too bad I had no damned idea what the hell to do with it. That was okay though because truth be told, my higher self and soul were absolutely leading the way energetically from within, helping me to start shifting my outer world.

Time went by, I kept hanging out with the new amazing influential Emma, and growing with my very soul-aligned partner, Joel. Things in life started to keep shifting in this positive direction. My partner and I finally got our own place, and I was evolving as a great manager at my job. I started meeting some new friends that loved to talk about space, life, being cosmic, and being "more than a walking meatsuit", as me and my best friend, Rachel would say all the time.

My best friend now, Rachel, is who came along my path and shifted my focus to the importance of connecting to my higher power by opening myself to more of the metaphysical world. Rachel is also the third human catalyst in my spiritual journey. The openness of these conversations, and this desire to connect to my spiritual side, led to me discovering the documentary "The Secret," on a day off as I was endlessly scrolling Netflix. The documentary made me feel the same way the book Marked did when I saw it on the shelf all those years before. So, I clicked play. However, little did I know that I was not just clicking play on the film that day. Soon I realized I was also clicking play on the expansion of my spiritual awakening.

I learned all about the law of attraction that day and that was when I got the answer as to how and what I needed to do to have more of what I wanted in life. So, I began cutting off friends that only used me for what I had and the parties I threw. I started watching how I talked to people about myself and how I talked about others. Most importantly, I started becoming more conscious of what I was thinking, feeling, doing, and saying. I changed everything up. I also immediately went to the library to get the book The Secret that followed the documentary.

I started adding meditation to my daily routine, setting goals regularly, healing myself as I got triggered, journaling about my feelings and thoughts, and learning about spirituality and my human self. That was the moment my reality finally shifted to being mine to create with purpose and intention. It has led me to be the spiritually awakened person I am now. To me, being spiritually awakened is about leaning into the, "Oh shit!" moments of my timeline and being in a scientist's mindset to play with my reality as I continuously hypothesize about what could be, given the connection I have between mind, body, self, and soul.

Now, in the present moment, I know anything can exist. I know I am truly an abundant creation source. I now get to follow my heart to what I truly desire. I am a holistic leadership coach helping people understand their own awakenings and seeing what can truly be done with that insight of the inside of the relationship between themselves and everything in (and out) of this world. I have a relationship full of love, growth focus, honesty, fun, and openness. I have friends that are absolutely out of this world. I am an energetic being having an awesome human experience, thanks to my spiritual awakening, and thanks to getting to see my potential and abilities.

With the spiritual awakening comes some side effects. I experienced a lot of self-sabotage and imposter syndrome, which I called my existential crisis. A lot of my spiritual awakening felt like an existential crisis because it came with a lot of breakdowns that would lead to world-shattering breakthroughs. Literally.

To go from seeing myself as a traumatized kid raised with shit conditions to BEING a cosmically confident being that is consciously manifesting major life goals, like moving from my hometown to a city full of opportunity, and meeting amazing soul-aligned people.

The awakening process got tough many times. It's not like when you wake up to get up out of bed to start the day. Some days it was like ripping a band-aid off a hairy arm and then having someone slap the sore spot right after. However, it has become beautiful as I have continued to be more aware and awakened to what is shifting and happening around me. I have become more conscious of my energetic role in circumstances as they continue to unfold.

I live now as the lead creative authority of my reality, all thanks to having a spiritual awakening. At times it was rough, and I felt like there was no way that the things I was going through were happening to help me expand, however, the energetic desire and intentions were there from within always. My spiritual awakening has allowed me to become conscious of that so that when negativity inevitably comes my way, I know how to connect my mind, body, and soul as one to help me make decisions. I think, feel, and respond in ways that allow me to be the one creating the outcomes I want.

My spiritual awakening has allowed me to see how I have been a marked one all along with my own magical powers. The journey has its ups and downs and honestly only gets deeper with time. The journey got scary at times because it was weird at first to get comfortable with the idea that my mind and heart could mold matter and completely change my world around me. The awakening process isn't just a process that happens, it's a way of living to me. It can be easy to get caught up in the surface level of things, the hustle and bustle culture, and go right back to being closed off energetically and mentally. Therefore, each day I make it a point to do things that get me spiritually activated, so I can continue to be in touch with myself, the universe, the earth, the land, the seas, people, and all other energetic sources around me on a deeper level.

I do meditation daily now to stay activated. When I say, "mediate," that does not always look like eyes closed, breathing in and out. Daily meditation for me is about connecting with my spirit, my soul, and my higher self so that I can honor my wants and needs! It's my time to be with myself and lean more into a balanced state of clarity to achieve what I desire.

I continue to invest in my learning for all areas of my life, including my mindset, healing modalities, my spiritual gifts, my physical health and bettering it in holistic ways, my emotional intelligence, and all my human components like money management, communication, and more tangible (less metaphysical) things. I also regroup and make space and time for integration. Regrouping allows for self-reflection which allows for deeper self-awareness, and deeper self-awareness leads to a deeper connection to all parts of self within and outside of the individuated spirit.

The integration time allows me to be present. Once awakened, I realized how it's counterintuitive to be working so intentionally towards achieving major life goals; when I do achieve them, I am not allowing myself the space to enjoy them completely or allowing my spirit and meatsuit to marinate in my intentionally created reality. So, the integration time weekly, or even daily, allows me to reflect and really experience my own life creations. This strengthens my intentions, intuition, and insights that I use to keep connecting and growing.

All these steps are ways I get aligned, especially as I work toward my "what's next," now. I intend to continue building a like-minded community online and start shifting to in-person community gatherings as well. These gatherings help people create more solutions spiritually and holistically by deepening the relationships they have with their mind, body, soul, and surroundings through energy healing, my self-empowered healing pyramid process, and creating unique soul-aligned habits. It's my desire to help others use their own awakening to live a soulful life. To do so I desire to be in tune with myself on a soul level continuously and create a more aligned and interconnected sense of self to be able to have healthy energetic boundaries.

The horizon for me is full of opportunity. I see a very near future with me surrounded by my true soul family members that geek out about life and the beyond while making a positive impact, and living off the land and all its natural resources. Continuing to do what genuinely lights me up from within is my choice, and this way of life is all thanks to a spiritual awakening.

It is crazy that two words could have such an abundant impact on life. The process was a lot like the Marked series I read. I was awakened to being marked, being gifted; leading to me being more awakened to my, and everyone else's, hidden abilities. These gifts can be revealed and redeemed by each and every one of us, as we step into the leadership role of self and soul, as we all have the cosmic birthright to be.

No matter where anyone is in their journey of being, feeling, and living awakened, I think it's important to transcend awareness, consistently be leaning into self-discovery, and heal old wounds. Most importantly on my path, I had to deepen the relationship I had with myself in order to create more alignment in my life, and understand that I was in charge of my own happiness and fulfillment, no matter the past or future circumstances that I have or might face. Life is ever revolving as we are ever-evolving.

The spiritual awakening tip that helped me the most was, "take the effort to continue to get to know yourself." Even as I evolve, I always come back to this, so that I am awake and aware of my abundant ability to create my reality. All the tools are accessible anywhere, anytime, thanks to the universe and all its metaphysical and tangible earthly gifts all around me, from the herbs that grow naturally in the ground, to the moonlight that charges my soul, and all things in between. I'm grateful for the epic humans around me that support me now, in the future, and most importantly my own inner knowing and energy.

It's all about continuing to gain insight to the inside of my reality and beyond, as a human and an abundant energetic source. Time to live, love, and rock 'n roll, while unleashing the best within infinity.

Lyndy Perez

"The fear of Death follows from the fear of Life. A man who lives fully is prepared to die at any time."

-Mark Twain

Fear is a bully. Fear is a primordial emotion that has been embedded within our DNA for eons. It is our natural alarm that alerts us when danger is near; whether seen or unseen. Fear was useful for early man as he wandered, hunted, and lived in the open wilderness among predatory beasts. It was, and still is, a useful emotion to ensure our survival, safety, and well-being. However, when we fast forward several millennia to the present day, many of us exist with fear as the dominant emotion in our day-to-day lives, hindering us from living at our true potential.

I was conditioned from early childhood to fear many things. I had a fear of water, fear of speaking, fear of abandonment or being alone, fear of the unseen, fear of the unfamiliar, fear of rejection, fear of pain, fear of conflict, and fear of death... just to name a few. These fears I carried with me far into my adulthood, and I soon developed unhealthy behaviors and coping mechanisms to bury those fears.

I became chronically depressed and anxious and as a result, found myself soothing or numbing my fears with unhealthy eating habits, alcohol, and prescription painkillers. Fear dominated every aspect of my life as I continually sought to run away from it instead of facing it. That's the thing, fear is relentless, and it soon caught up with me. Just like a bully, fear did not stop until I confronted it, and that is where my story of awakening unfolds...

It was 2016 when, after decades of figuratively running from myself and my poor life choices, my body started saying, "No more." By that time I was 44 years old, seven years into a second marriage that was crumbling apart, burned out, severely depressed, suffering from frequent bouts of migraines, peri-menopausal symptoms like hot flashes, night sweats, mood swings, and chronic fatigue. Years earlier I had already suffered from several mental breakdowns, the first one occurring soon after leaving my first husband in 2007; that one forced me, courtesy of law enforcement, into a three-day stay in a psych ward at a local hospital. Between 2008 and 2015 I suffered multiple mental breakdowns, each episode forcing me to take months off from work on stress leave. By 2015 the life I had so unskillfully tried to hold together was unraveling rapidly.

In late 2016, I decided to visit my OBGYN for ongoing painful periods, which often times compelled me to take an absence from work. In addition, it was becoming more and more painful to have intercourse with my spouse, so much so that sex was no longer enjoyable. Tests showed that I had fibroids, endometriosis, adenomyosis, ovarian cysts, an inflamed cervix, and a thickened lining of the uterus which the doctor suspected at first could potentially be uterine cancer. Later biopsies confirmed it was not cancer, but I did need a total hysterectomy; everything had to go, uterus, ovaries, both fallopian tubes, and my cervix.

The surgery was set for the end of January 2017. This was my first time having any kind of surgery and I was frightened. I had heard tragic stories of patients dying due to complications from surgery, but it just wasn't the fear of dying I had to face, I suddenly became insecure that my value as a woman would diminish because I would no longer be able to bare a child. I was already heartbroken that my marriage was falling apart, but this procedure would, in my opinion, just make me even more undesirable toward my husband. The surgery took place on January 25. When I woke up afterward, I was thankful to have survived going under the knife. Recovery would take 8 weeks, and I was encouraged by my doctor to begin HRT (hormone replacement therapy) because my body was now forced into an instant menopause due to the hysterectomy. Reluctantly I agreed.

On March 19th of 2017, I was due to see my OBGYN surgeon for a post-operation follow-up visit. Healing from the hysterectomy was painful but without complications. That afternoon as I was sitting on the floor of my apartment playing with my beloved dog, Bailey when suddenly I felt intense itchiness above the nipple of my left breast. As I proceeded to scratch that area my fingers touched a very large, hardened lump in the area. What was this?! Was this lump always there? My instincts told me this was highly abnormal. I would compare the size, shape, and hardness of the newly discovered lump to that of an Oreo cookie. Perfectly round and dense. I thought if the growth was there before the surgery, then surely I would have noticed it! When I saw my OBGYN I immediately told him about the unusual growth. At first, he dismissed it as something benign. "Oh, it's probably nothing, just take an over-the-counter iodine pill and it will go away," he said unconcernedly. My blood started to boil at his confident diagnosis despite not having done tests at all. Stubbornly, I refused to leave his office until he ordered diagnostic tests and biopsies.

Another two months passed before I was able to get the biopsies and diagnostic mammogram. Finally, on June 1st, I received the phone call that I didn't want. The doctor's nurse called me at work around 10 a.m. and requested I see the doctor at his office that day. I will tell you, no good news ever comes when a doctor requests to see you the same day. I called my husband, and after meeting him at home, we drove together to the medical office. My husband and I were waiting silently in the doctor's office. I wanted to run out of there. I was feeling anxious and frightened because deep in my gut I knew that this was going to be the news that NOBODY is ever prepared to hear. The doctor then entered the exam room somberly and quietly, as if someone had died. "I have the results," he said. My husband and I were silent. "You have breast cancer." At that moment, I will tell you that my initial reaction was to punch the wall, but instead, I pursed my lips, clenched my fist tightly, and calmly said, "What do we need to do next to take care of this?"

That afternoon, the car ride home was silent. As we neared our apartment, I impulsively directed my husband to take me to our usual restaurant because I needed to process what I had just heard, over beer and buffalo wings, my favorite comfort meal. The predominant emotion I felt that day was anger. Not sadness, but boiling, seething, raging ANGER. I had still been recovering from the hysterectomy I'd had just a few months earlier while still coming to terms with the fact that I could no longer bear a child, and now THIS. This new possibility that I would lose my breast. That I would have to endure more pain. Endure more pieces being cut out of me. Endure more poisons to "cure" me. I felt like the bully, Fear, was once again terrorizing me. This time it felt like Death had surely set his arrow toward me.

People have fears. It is natural. Some fears are irrational, like the fear of heights, fear of darkness, fear of crowds, or fear of small spaces, because the probability of being killed or injured, although not zero, is minuscule. Cancer is another thing. Your own body is trying to kill you. Rapidly. It's the ultimate betrayal. You against you. I cried for 5 days straight after I got the news. I refused to speak to anyone. I retreated to the bedroom and cried. My husband didn't know how to take the news, after all, I was the strong one in this marriage. I was the strong one among my friends. Now here I was facing the possibility of death. When you are the rock for everyone in your circle and then suddenly you are not... your friends will not know how to react. Some will fall away from fear. Stay silent. Feel lost. My husband was one of them. In those 5 days, not once did he come to my side. He did not lie down with me. I did not receive hugs or encouraging words from him. Our apartment was silent as if Death had already taken residence with us.

Death became familiar to me at a young age. Like most of us, I have lost loved ones, friends, relatives, and pets. It was when my boyfriend committed suicide when I was 19 and he was 21, that I truly experienced profound loss. But when cancer finally gripped its malicious hand in my body, it is at that time I became painfully aware that this version of me HAD to die.

I was into a second marriage that was becoming cold. My corporate career of 15 years had depleted my vitality. All of this unhappiness, or dis-ease, had physically manifested itself into aggressive cancer growing inside me. It had to go; my old Life, the sick, unhealthy, and depressed version of me, all of it. Cancer, in an ironic way, changed my course trajectory. I finally admitted that I was not living true to myself. I had married a second time because I was afraid of being alone. I stayed in it, or rather tolerated the dysfunction of it, for 8 years, and I had to admit to myself that I had not ever given myself the self-compassion I desperately needed, but rather I spent decades seeking it outside of myself. Self-Love. Healing. Yes, this is what I needed to learn from cancer.

I had always been considered by my friends, as well as strangers even, as a source of wisdom, guidance, and healing. Yet here I was pouring outward onto others without ever having considered pouring love inward into myself. Cancer stopped me in my tracks and gave me a strong knock over the head. My own body rebelled against me because it KNEW I was on a path of self-annihilation.

It took two years to fight this cancer. ten rounds of chemo infusions, eight hours each session. Thirty consecutive days of radiation, and being opened up under the surgical knife again, this time to remove the tumor that the chemo successfully shrunk. During those 80 hours spent on the chemo chair, I had plenty of time to contemplate my life thus far. I had never truly understood what self-love and living true to myself meant until my life was in serious peril.

As a young college girl, my career trajectory was pointed toward art and design. However, that all was buried away when my boyfriend committed suicide. That young girl, me, was buried with him because I felt responsible for his death. I was so involved with my studies and creative projects that I failed to recognize his pleas for help. After that tragic event, I decided to take the safe route. I married a doctor and lived a safe life as a housewife. I killed all my dreams and creativity and poured my entire being into keeping my young doctor spouse happy... except he wasn't happy. No matter what I did to cater to his needs it was never enough. We lasted ten years. As soon as I finalized my divorce with the doctor, I jumped immediately to dating husband #2, without allowing myself time to heal from the previous heartbreak. My second marriage also lasted ten years. Twenty years spent pouring my love onto others but never pouring love into myself.

During and after cancer treatment, I made earnest efforts to FINALLY create my own path, one of creative expression while still being of service to others. Despite my inability to create human life, I still had the power and vision to create art. Despite the painful experience of two failed marriages and a near-death experience from breast cancer and cancer treatment, when all seemed destroyed... it was at that moment I had a breakthrough: I CAN still create a different life for myself. After all, I SURVIVED. I can design and live life on my own terms and help guide others to do the same.

As I wrote this, I was sitting in a cafe, eating a croissant, sipping on hot coffee with a dash of creamer, gratefully recounting the trials I endured to learn self-love and compassion. In 2022 I fought and conquered yet another type of cancer that was even more aggressive than the first. This time it was a rare form of sarcoma. This second cancer, the sarcoma, was such that my left breast had to be removed by a mastectomy. My hair has grown back from chemo now, the scar from the hysterectomy has fully healed, and the mastectomy scar is healing as well. While you are reading this, there has been, yet another tumor detected in my body. Could this possibly be a third bout of cancer? Who knows. I patiently wait for my doctor to do tests in two weeks. Perhaps fighting cancer is not over yet. I will keep getting back up. I will keep on my trajectory as Creatrix, the artist, mentor, guide, and facilitator for those willing to shift their life path.

The beauty of duality, the loss and gain, sickness and health, or life and death, is that you cannot know of one without the other. It took multiple battles with cancer for me to learn how to embrace life and respect death. These days, I walk with gratitude and an open heart, despite all the reasons why I should contract and close up to life's wonderful possibilities.

Allison Barnett

In my fifty years here on earth, I have come to two solid conclusions when it comes to spirituality. The first is that spirituality is a beautiful journey filled with the utmost mind-fuckery known to man. The second is that God, Jesus, Buddha, and all their friends, are easiest to find in hospitals and jail cells. But before we get into how I've come to these fabulous conclusions, let me introduce myself. I'm Allison Barnett, an Intuitive Realtor, who grew up thinking life was a simple path of rules, schools, marriage, friends, and work. Apparently, this was the one time I probably should have taken a closer look at the user manual, because it turns out that the cliff notes really skipped some major points; the kind that will literally send you into a tailspin and wonder if you will ever get right side up.

For me, it starts in Brooklyn, New York, with my mom, dad, an older sister, and a serious roster of grandparents, aunts, uncles, and cousins, some of whom I still don't know. I had middle class, both parents working, I was totally adored, blah blah blah. In fact, I'm told I was a calm baby who didn't cry much, so thumbs up on the launch of me earth-side! Other than expecting a boy, my parents set the stage for a happy little life that should fit any paint-by-numbers storyline.

My primary years were spent on Long Island, where I had the coolest teachers ever! My older sister had boring, structured teachers, so my mom picked the fun ones for me. I'm pretty sure that Mother's Intuition probably warned her that her second child would be an elementary school dropout if I had to do research papers in third grade. So, instead, I had a blast freestyling my way through school. God Bless Mrs. Gallucci, who dared to take a first-grade class into her home to make vegetable soup together and meet her big dogs before we all bundled up to play on the icy lake. Seriously, this happened! Mind you, it was back in a time when we also went home for lunch because no one wanted to eat sandwiches when we could talk our parents into pizza.

We lived in a safe area, with not much crime or drama... it was normal for us kids to disappear for hours, just checking in when we needed to. I had no concept of money other than to recognize that there were big houses and small houses... we were, of course, in the middle, with nice neighbors and a short walk to school where kids joined each other along the way and parents may or may not have followed.

And the holidays! The holidays were all kinds of amazing. Jewish holidays, Thanksgiving, Chanukkah, and Christmas AKA bonus Chanukkah, were spent in part at my grandparent's house, packed full of people, food, laughter, and arguments. So much magic and celebration in the air. It was probably my first concept of a vibe. The holiday family vibe is the one I lived for! I still swear that a Santa or two may have had some hidden angel wings because their eyes seem to sparkle way more than everyone else's.

Looking back, it was picture-perfect. Sickness, divorce, addiction... these concepts weren't anything I was aware of. Yes, shit happened, but it wasn't as commonplace as it is like today. So, other than eating a few too many Twinkies that wiggled when we jiggled, a broken bone was the extent of the drama. Until it wasn't... because my broken leg started a series of life-changing events, that in hindsight, probably sparked my spiritual journey.

Ice skating is a blast...especially when it's just me and my dad and you add in some hot cocoa. Of course, the cocoa was too hot, so I decided to skate a little longer while mine cooled off. Except that a few brilliant moves turned into a trip to the emergency room. A full leg cast later, I had my first hint of the Universe at work. Thank goodness my dad was there to carry me, and we had a Volkswagen van that fit my big-ass cast because the Pinto sure wouldn't have! Funny how those things just happened to work out, right?! But I had no clue back then...

That broken leg triggered my scoliosis. Thank goodness they were testing in 3rd grade, because at that time standard testing was performed in 5th grade... Of course, at the time, I wasn't so thankful. It was a miserable road of back braces, doctors, chiropractors, and even being the human test subject for what is now known as a tens machine.

Did you catch the mention of chiropractors? Well, my plight awakened new dreams for my dad. His newfound desire to become a chiropractor required packing up our now family of five and moving to Georgia, AKA, the bible belt. Was it fate? Destiny? Coincidence?! Whatever you call it, this was an obvious and unique chain of events that changed the trajectory of our lives.

Welcome to the South! If it were cool to say back then, this would be a major OMG moment! Who knew that religion was a whole identity?! I mean, I grew up with a bunch of Jewish kids who were friends with the Catholic kids... but in the South, religion is like fast food! There is a church on every corner and each one has its own menu of beliefs! Like, "Footloose is REAL!" There really are people who don't dance or drink or swear! And meeting new neighbors consisted of names and church invitations, with a side eye of just making sure you do go to church. Bless their hearts, this northern Jewish family definitely caused a stir!

Silly me, I'd thought everyone believed in God and that the rest didn't matter. I loved going to church with friends in New York. There was this big bazaar we'd go to afterward where we bought toys and junk. It was great! But in the South, church is Church and the one you belong to will also identify your friends. It is an organization. A club. You belong or you don't, though I'm told, "Everyone is welcome." To this day, I honestly still don't get it.

I remember being asked if I had horns. For real. I also remember that tearful day when my friend informed me that God told her that we could no longer be friends because of my faith. My uncle encouraged me to ask her for God's phone number so he could have a chat, haha. This was when I began to realize that religion and spirituality were quite different, though, to me, they felt the same.

Now, as an adult, I believe that religion and spirituality are very different, though they can easily be combined. In the simplest of terms, religion is structure. It is rules, regimens, and traditions. Spirituality is connection. A relationship with a higher power, the world at large, and each other. Spiritual connections are soul level, while religion is more human and cognizant. I am still Jewish, but my spirituality... well, that is an ever-growing connection thanks to life and all its lessons.

They say bad things happen in threes. I'm sure you can always find the pattern if you look hard enough. But when my father passed away, I had that moment of "I knew it!" because I had lost both of my grandfathers two years prior; so year three was my biggest loss, my dad, and from where I stand now, I believe he had to have known it too.

On a spring day, my older sister and I were leaving on a trip to Orlando with the high school band. My mom was working, so my dad was there to see us off. The buses were loaded and about to leave when suddenly, my dad hops onto the bus to give us another hug. His smile was so big. He was so proud. And that was the last time I saw my dad walk this earth.

While in Orlando, before receiving the news, my friends and I were hanging out with our bandmates. Our band was big enough that some kids we only knew as acquaintances. Yet, that day, one of those acquaintances became a friend, and he is now my husband of 25 years. He was there when my sister and I received the news. He attended the funeral. He was the one to dry many of my tears and wound up being the only guy I ever dated.

Did my dad know that he was really saying goodbye when he came to give us that one last hug? Did he know that he was leaving me in good hands? Did God arrange all of this? If you have any level of spirituality, you stop believing in coincidences, so you know it's a yes.

Our Rabbi said that my father was still around, but living on a different plane of existence, where we can't see or touch him, yet he would always be with us, hear us, and watch over us. I totally thought he was full of crap. I hated visiting the cemetery and prayed that I could have one more conversation with my dad... just one. It took 20 years to realize that the Rabbi was right. I just had to stay on this journey of life and spirituality to see it.

Married life was fabulous, being young, clueless, and broke. We adopted a dog. We had a cute home. Happy times except for the sudden decline of my husband's health that no one could identify. It took two years to find out that my husband, Knox, has Rheumatoid Arthritis (RA). A beast of a chronic illness that took way too long to diagnose. It was like hell on earth, on our marriage, and nothing that life had prepared me for. Seeing someone in so much pain!

All the time! In my twenties! Ugh! Thank goodness we decided to add Knox to my health insurance that year!

The day we finally had answers about his health issues, I went to Barnes and Noble, purchased $300 in books, and told Knox that I would cure him. Yes, I said it. No, I had no medical knowledge and barely passed biology, but something in me was not willing to just let this be handled by doctors. So, the research began, and we were fortunate to have an amazing doctor that was open to all my questions and suggestions. Thank goodness!

A friend introduced me to Prevention magazine, one of those mini magazines from the grocery store that everyone reads while waiting to check out. It was months before I bought one, but there was an irresistible pasta recipe that I just had to try, so I grabbed it. Funny how the magazine that I saw a zillion times suddenly became a priority and just happened to have an advertisement for a book about curing inflammation through diet; a book that would end up literally saving my husband's life! No way can that ever be considered a coincidence. After all, I did randomly say that I would cure him. Within weeks of receiving this book, we kicked that RA into remission, reduced Knox's medications within months, and to this day, flares are still rare, and medications are still minimal. Thank goodness!

Today, I am VERY aware that I was the catalyst, that God provided the path, and that Knox took the aligned action for this healing miracle. I know this because, at the very same time that I was recognizing all these coincidences and healing my husband, I was also binging on all things Sylvia Brown, the psychic. I absolutely loved her and really wanted to have some of her gifts. I mean, I could help the world and myself, and truly, I already was.

It was 2008, the construction industry was crashing, and my real estate job went with it. Money was tight, life was stressful, and I was praying for miracles. I suspected that I had just miscarried our first baby. I was desperate for answers, doctors sucked, and a friend who claimed to be psychic wouldn't leave me in peace. She introduced me to her friend, another psychic. My skepticism kicked in when she nailed everything about me since there was a slight chance that my friend had clued her in. Yet, when she started telling me all kinds of stuff about my husband, I had that, "Oh shit, this is real," lightbulb moment. There was no way she could have known that information. I was hooked!

I started studying the law of attraction. I started seeing signs from the Universe everywhere. I practiced being conscious of my words and thoughts, and then, it happened... the ultimate sign that I couldn't have made up if I wanted to. In the middle of the night, I dreamt that my dad was with me. It's rare that I ever dream about him, but when I do, it's the most peaceful feeling, like he tucks me in and kisses my forehead. When I felt the kiss, I looked at the clock, and the time was precisely the same number as my birthday. In an instant, I knew that the connection was real. My dad was really with me at that moment. Talk about being excited! I couldn't wait to tell Knox! But his response floored me. HE had also had a dream about my dad, and when Knox looked at the clock, he saw the exact same time that I did, yet we weren't awake together!

To be extra clear, I received the most obvious, amazing, still-gives-me-chills-to-tell-story kind of sign that my dad visits me. That he is still around and communicating in a way that I now know to be him. The Rabbi was right!

It was a boost of energy so huge that my intuition went into overdrive! I started receiving more signs as my faith and intuitive awareness grew. It was incredible. Amid these wonderous spiritual events, life was still darn hard. Money, fertility, trying to refinance our house during a housing crash... it was a mess. I was on a mission; I just knew there was a way to fix it all. I knew that I was one step away from making the magic happen. I just needed to find it. So, I stayed the course and let it find me.

Obsessed, I attended every psychic fair and gathering that my psychic friends had. I was told to rewrite my story AKA beliefs, to have faith, and let go (insert eye roll). All these words made sense in theory, yet they obviously weren't working, because I was still struggling! So, I prayed, affirmed, and cleared energy leaks. I kept asking for more help, and more signs. I learned to read my own tarot and trust my own instincts. I went to healers. I began to shift energy. I even asked God for more gifts. I mean, why not?! I was still working on manifesting a baby and needed all the help I could get!

Note to self: be careful what you wish for! When I created my first intention sigil, which is an intention made into artform to amplify the energy, holy chaos erupted! Hysterical and in tears, I called a friend begging for help to reverse whatever I had done because my wish for financial freedom went totally awry! Suddenly, my home needed thousands in repairs, Knox, blew a tire, my dog was sick, and my bank account was almost empty!

She laughed. A lot. Then she congratulated me on collapsing time. The Universe apparently condensed months or years of hiccups into a short week, clearing the path to achieve my dreams faster. Who knew that this was even a thing?! But it is... and I can do it. I'm a powerful manifester, and yet I still don't have everything I want. Is this one of life's little ironies? Am I being too greedy? Is the Universe just determined to teach me every lesson in one lifetime? Maybe I'm not grateful enough.

I made the decision to be extra grateful. My husband was healthy, my bills were paid, my dog was happy, and my life was on cruise control, kind of. Every night, I would journal my gratefulness and intuitively started to write down any messages that popped into my head... warnings, guidance, support, and ideas. The more I wrote, the more I received, and suddenly, I became a channeler. Watch out, Sylvia Brown!

But G-d has a sense of humor, and it's called Clairaudience. Those messages come in voice format, too. And when you are driving down the road, hearing an unknown voice answering your own thoughts, you freak out before realizing how cool it is to have a party in your head. When people say you are never alone, take it as the truth. FYI - visions may come next, because mine did. The party is in full swing and I am loving the divine connection!

The best way to describe my life is that I have the holy grail on a silver platter. Is life perfect? No. Do I still want more? Of course. But, I am a total badass at manifesting! I can channel guidance to coach clients in life and business. I can shift and clear energy blocks in people and homes – which works really well as a Realtor. My clients even think I walk on water, in the sense that I really do help them manifest some amazing feats. It's honestly pretty darn magical!

The journey isn't always easy. And while I can't officially confirm that God and his buddies hang out in hospitals and jail cells – they are definitely on call when shit has you sliding downhill faster than you can keep up. There really is calm in the storm, and miracles are just around the corner.

I am connected to a Universe far beyond my sight or understanding. I am part of a world that has tapped into a frequency that many will never grasp. The magic is flowing. Prayers are being answered. Real life is the spiritual awakening. We just have to open our eyes to see it. I did and it's one hell of a ride!

Jaime Zazzara

Spiritual Awakenings can be referred to as "enlightenment," reaching "nirvana," or a "state of bliss." It can also feel like a rebirth of the soul. For me, my journey to self-awareness began in 2012 with my network marketing side hustle. Who knew that ordering a Big Brown Box of nutritional products would align me with people, places, and events that would ultimately change the course of my life?

I believe many spiritual awakenings occur throughout our journey and that was the case with me. The awakening I will be sharing was rather significant because it had a ripple effect and forced me to change and step into my purpose and power by getting focused on my own healing. First, let me give you some background about my life before this...

In June of 2020, after covid had hit our nation, I was living in Fort Lauderdale with my partner of 5 years and my two boys, 17 and 12. We moved to Florida due to a job opportunity. At first, it gave us a new lease on life and a chance to start over after finalizing my divorce. I wanted nothing more than a happy family. It was amazing to have found a man who stepped in and up as stepdad, but the reality was that we connected with a trauma bond through the lens of our past wounds. It was very difficult living with kids and doing our best to co-parent with different parenting styles and his OCD. It quickly became a regular occurrence of yelling, upset feelings, and a battle within the roles of co-parenting. The mentality was his way or the highway, and he let it be known that we could just leave if we didn't adjust to his way of living.

A few years into the relationship, being isolated from my family back in New Jersey, he would emotionally abuse me on a daily basis, demean me, making me second guess myself and my ability to make decisions. He had such power and control over me. Eventually, I gave in and lost my voice. It wasn't worth the fight anymore to try to make my opinion heard. I didn't see how this man, who had stepped in as stepfather when my boys needed him, had become so abusive.

My children saw it and tried to do what was necessary to keep the peace. They tried to warn me, but I didn't want to see it or believe it. I kept adjusting my behavior to make him happy. He made me feel such shame and guilt, and overall, unworthy of love. I had attracted a man that I would never be enough for.

At this time, I was working with a business coach doing Core Wound Healing, which is a form of intensive inner work. I knew that we would not be able to be happy unless we both dealt with our past pain. Through this process, I was able to see all of our wounds and what we both needed to work through for ourselves. I poured my heart and soul into this writing process. When I shared this with him, he completely dismissed it. He thought I was crazy and didn't understand my process of healing.

On my birthday and we went for a weekend trip where the shit hit the fan. That's when I finally found my voice. I had this epiphany that I had once again become co-dependent and financially dependent on a man. There was so much pain and hurt on both sides.

We came back from the trip and got covid at the start of July 2020. It hit us pretty hard, and I see now that having covid was a huge part of the events that would unfold. It brought to the surface underlying conditions, and for me, it was my mental state. I had epilepsy from ages 5-to-30. After I had my first child, tests confirmed I no longer had epilepsy. However, my body had been dependent on medication for 25 years. About 2 years after I weaned off medication, I was diagnosed with Bipolar. The crazy thing is that epilepsy medication also treats Bipolar.

What happened with the process of Core Wound Healing opened me up in a way that I was not equipped to handle. Meanwhile, my partner was emotionally unavailable to help me and made it worse by the way he treated me. It was a perfect storm! I could see how every event in my life led me to where I was, and I could see his pain as well. I knew what had to be done, but he wasn't open to it, or ready to even acknowledge his part in our relationship. He became even angrier, and the arguing and fighting escalated while my children watched.

A few weeks after we got covid, we went to Vero Beach; I had a job interview. I fell in love with this beach town and the school I would be working for. I got the job and was ready to take the position even though I would be moving before my partner. While there, I had a few experiences that led to my awakening. First, I wanted to go paddleboarding in the ocean to reach a shipwreck off the shore called SS Birchenshire. It was symbolic of our journey. My partner snorkeled in a straight line towards the American Flag, the marker for the wreck. I started from a much further place going towards it in an L path.

We were both moving toward a shipwreck flag representing FREEDOM. We had to go our own way and persevere. It was the most treacherous ride I had ever experienced. The waves were strong, and I had to surrender. I felt like I was Tom Hanks in Castaway. I was talking to myself, "Just keep swimming, just keep swimming to get there." There was no way I could force or control my path. I had to completely surrender to the ebb and flow of the waves. I recall thinking of how similar this was to life. When you surrender and allow, life is filled with ease, instead of force and control. As I let go, I saw a fully grown adult sea turtle swim right by me. I knew this was a sign to let go and be in full surrender to God.

That night, there was a horrific lightning storm that lit up the sky from our ocean view room. I was talking on the phone and every time I said the word HEAL, the sky lit up like a Christmas tree. I knew God was showing me my power. I knew this was one more sign for me to step into my purpose. I couldn't sleep and got up for sunrise. I was in a state of complete hysteria, crying and releasing. I had this intensely strong energy course through me. My hands felt completely numb, and I couldn't shake the feeling. I knew God was coming through me once again for me to wake up and serve my purpose in the world. I made a commitment that no matter what I would serve my higher purpose and tap into my intuition. I spent an hour at the beach that morning alone trying to understand what was happening. That intense energy was so strong and felt like what is described as a Kundalini Awakening.

That experience changed me, and I was not "acting like myself." On one hand, I was finally seeing my life with such clarity. On the other hand, my relationship was crumbling before my eyes. My emotions were heightened, and I couldn't handle them. The next morning, I woke up to visions of my ex in pain as a child. I knew he needed to heal. My mind was so much in the clouds that I needed to ground myself. I had barely been sleeping anyways, so I got up and left to go to the beach to ground myself. While there, I had a few conversations with people, and I could see and feel their pain. I was in a complete state of channeling for a few people, much like a Psychic Empath, as I walked by them. I didn't understand what was happening. All I knew was that I was no longer going to be scared of my gift.

On my way home, I witnessed my rebirth in a vision of my father looking like an angel above my mother and me. I came into this world in fear and in a traumatic way. I was seeking to understand why I had epilepsy and wondered if I had been born differently, would my life have been different? I could see that my older son also came into the world in fear as that was where I was emotionally at the time of his birth. This in turn caused him to experience trauma and pain in his life.

When I got home, everyone was looking for me and was worried because I had been gone for a long time. I was so tired but the first thing I did was go to my son and tell him he was going to be OK and that he didn't have to live with anxiety and pain. My behavior was abnormal to them, and I was acting erratic, not of sound mind.

Just as I was about to rest in my bed, a loud knock came from the front porch. It was the police. My older son had called 911 because he saw me needing help and he didn't know what to do. My younger son came with me to the front porch and stayed by my side the entire time. My partner was nowhere to be found either. The police thought there was a domestic dispute. The cops wanted to take me to the hospital, but I didn't want to go. I remember sitting down and showing them I was calm and would cooperate. They didn't listen and ultimately handcuffed me, and placed a Baker Act on me, which is a 3-day suicide watch.

Doctors refer to what happened to me as psychosis, which led me to the hospital for 4 days to reset and process what had occurred. I had a manic episode which was very traumatic for my children and me. My mind and body were unequipped to handle the intensity of energy that passed through me. It turned out I still had covid, so I spent two days in the ER and then they moved me to the ICU. I knew I had to completely surrender and the only way out of this situation was to heal. I brought a teddy bear with me and while in the hospital, I experienced another rebirth. I visualized Jack being reborn when he was supposed to. God knew I needed to rest my mind and get back to neutral. On day 4, doctors released me, and I continued on medication that made me feel numb. This episode would lead me to go back to New Jersey where I could be around family and heal.

Since July 2020, I have held onto such guilt and shame, feeling embarrassed for my behavior and the aftermath effects. I had Covid, was not in my right mind, and experienced a rebirth, and an awakening that would change the course of my life.

This is what I have learned after my awakening: I am not here to heal others. I am here to heal myself. I thought I could heal my ex so we could be happy in our relationship. I always felt I was meant for some BIGGER purpose. I could finally see the power I had within me and knew God put me on this planet to serve a much bigger purpose than I could ever imagine. I also know that I would not be able to serve his purpose if I didn't experience some pretty challenging things in my life. It is knowing that I had to see and feel the depths of darkness and lows for me to see the contrast, as Esther Hicks describes. It is in the contrast that you can see the light.

I have described myself as shining my light so bright it blinds people and allows me to reach new heights. Then, I stop and surrender and put a complete halt on my beautiful light. Like a turtle, I retreat into my shell, scared and living in fear of actually showing my true self to the world. This happened because the people around me didn't understand me and made me feel like I could not step into who I am. Fear of not being accepted, fear of not being worthy, living with the uncertainty of people wanting what I have to offer. There is so much that I have experienced that I felt I had to deal with and move on from.

But what if I am the one to go first? What if I had to learn these life lessons and experiences about myself, about life, about purpose, about loss, about grief, forgiveness, pain, shame, and guilt? We all come into this life to experience those lessons so we can find love, joy, passion, purpose, happiness, and peace of mind.

Since being back in New Jersey, I have spent two years focused on my own healing, using techniques including therapy, Reiki energy healing, Hypnosis to release past trauma, and spiritual counseling, all supporting my goal to release any pain, fear, and trauma that is holding me back.

GUS, God/Universe/Source, has smacked me right in the face with curve balls and experiences where I had to surrender and change. I choose to let go, forgive, become self-aware, and understand that all the events in my life have led me to the here and now. I focus on surrendering to my higher power as I know I am not meant to see the big picture just yet. My job is simply to focus on what I desire in my life, not how it will come to me.

In doing this, I have been fully supported by the universe, bringing me people that I require on my path to align with my higher purpose. I am just now stepping into my gift as a healer, letting go of anyone else's expectations or judgment of who I am. It feels absolutely amazing knowing I am serving my purpose.

I don't know exactly what it will eventually look like, but what I do know for sure is that it is all unfolding in the most magical way! As I feel the world around me, I know I am meant to go first, for me to be the change I wish to see in the world. I am supposed to rise above the chaos and share vulnerably so others can do the same. There are too many people suffering, lost, blind, and not understanding how life is meant to be lived. We are not meant to be here on this planet to live in fear, shame, or guilt.

LOVE is the highest vibration and I know I am meant to teach others how to get back to a place of love. I am OPEN and READY to receive all that God has in store for me. I no longer fear my gifts and my power to heal others on their own path. I look forward to connecting and serving my purpose in divine timing.

Melissa Conkling

Spiritual Awakening. The truth is, I don't love the term. I believe each one of us is born "awoken", but we lose, or more accurately, forget about, this innate connection as our conscious mind and ego evolve. We begin to allow fear to take over, sometimes in the most subtle of ways. It's what I experienced throughout my life, and I see it in countless people in all areas of my life.

I couldn't tell you precisely when the fear began for me. I simply know that it wasn't always there, but over time, it came to silently control nearly everything in my life without me even being aware of it for decades. While I was always shy and precocious, famously meowing at strangers my parents would introduce me to, I distinctly remember that being my unique way of resisting expectations. Perhaps I'm wrong, but I simply don't believe fear was the culprit behind my shyness. In fact, I remember always feeling incredibly safe throughout my childhood. Unfortunately, this is not something everyone can say. It is something I have taken for granted, I'm sure, but I always felt safe. Safe with my family, safe to be me, safe in the world, and most importantly, safe in nature.

Nature was always where I felt most at home. When other kids spent their weekends at slumber parties, playing video games, or doing whatever the "normal" kids did, my weekends and afternoons were quite often spent with my dad at the tree farm. While my dad would be planting, mowing, or shearing trees, I would be off in the woods playing. Most often in the grove of trees my sister and I named, the enchanted forest, searching for the fairies, determined to find the source of the mysterious sounds and magical spirits I could always sense in the woods.

There was an innately spiritual element to the tree farm, though I didn't know it as "spiritual" at the time. Rather, I saw it as magical. There was a power there that many people, especially my dad, experienced often. It revealed itself in mystical, otherworldly ways, like the overgrown tree my dad would no longer shear because he saw it glowing on some evenings, though lab tests showed nothing out of the ordinary about the tree. A mysterious and irresistible force drew him to the massive oak tree that stood at the edge of my enchanted forest and that made him nervous. Events like these just happened there.

That magic can still be felt. Visiting the tree farm last year for the first time in decades, I realized as an adult how different the air is there. It's as though the spiritual elements of nature live actively in this plot of land. This magic lived inside me as well, as a spiritual side that grew throughout my life just under the surface. It made me feel safe, as though the world itself was always looking out for me.

At some point in what I now estimate to be my middle school years, however, the sense of safety began to give way and fear took over. Not a noticeable, anxiety-filled fear, just a cloud that wasn't there beforehand. Perhaps that's how it was able to get such a strong grip on me. There was no glaringly obvious event or disruption in my life, no drastic change in me that sent up the warning signals, and so it went unnoticed by all, especially me.

As hanging out with friends on the weekends became more prevalent than going to the farm with my dad, my time in nature changed. I grew up in a small town with lots of woods, so I could never claim it lessened, but what was once my private world of spirits and fairies, and imagination was now shared with others. I began to hold back, only truly letting my mind flow when I was by myself in the woods behind our house.

In those woods though, things were different. The intrinsic spiritual energy of the tree farm only a half mile away was instead replaced by a feeling of danger and tragedy. Our home was part of an early

19th-century glass factory that burned down in a fire, leaving melted fragments of glass sprinkled throughout our land as a reminder of what happened there. The property also backed up to a hunting club. The silence of the woods was all too often shattered by the booming rifles of hunters who had wandered onto our property in pursuit of their prey, sending me running back home for cover in panic and anger.

Yes, nature felt different there. Life was different there. I became different there. Not only because of the old factory or the hunting club. Not only because the woods weren't as magical there. It was because we moved there the summer before I began middle school.

In a new home just five minutes down the road from our previous home, it seemed like I entered a different world. That feeling sealed itself in my mind before I even made it to school on the first day. Waiting at the end of our driveway with my older sister, we saw the school bus barreling down the hill at an unexpected speed. Certain it was going to pass us, at the last minute, the driver slammed on the brakes and screeched to a halt in front of us. The door folded open, and over the radio we heard the blasting music, "Welcome to the Jungle." The driver leaned towards us and shouted, "You girls going to school?" In shock, we nodded and boarded the bus.

If I wasn't nervous about middle school before that, after this I was terrified. Looking back, I suppose that is when a seed of fear planted itself inside my mind, waiting until the perfect time to come into full bloom. That day would arrive in the most unintended way in 7th grade, at the hands of my favorite teacher. He wasn't a "real" teacher though. He was a regular substitute. A retired, older man who could be found covering for one of my teachers on almost any given day. With less responsibility and less of a need to follow the rules, Mr. Breault talked to us like real people, rather than homework-producing, fact-spewing robots.

One day, Mr. Breault was on a bit of a rampage and began our math class with an impromptu lecture on the importance of authenticity. The class of 12- and 13-year-olds giggled nervously while they squirmed uncomfortably in their seats as he loudly pronounced, "There's only one person in this room who isn't constantly emulating someone else... and that's Melissa," and he pointed right at me.

All eyes turned in my direction, and I can only assume that my face turned a shade of red brighter than my hair... and I wanted to shrink. To hide under my desk. To disappear. I was proud... I knew I was original, but I didn't want everyone else to know too. My ability to pretend my uniqueness wasn't all that obvious was taken away. Now, if they hadn't realized it before, Mr. Breault's speech assured me that they all knew. So, I began to hide.

Over the years, I got better and better at hiding who I really was and trying harder to fit in until it became second nature. When you begin to hide your true self, it opens the door for fear to take over. High school and college became a blur of alternating periods of embracing my authenticity and hiding myself away. I began to release things that made me, Me; most significantly my love of and connection to nature. I was spending less time outdoors each year until it was practically nonexistent. It would be decades before my special time in nature and my spiritual connection was re-established.

Now, I understand that it's incredibly unlikely that you had the same upbringing as me. You, more likely than not, did not grow up in the presence of a Glowing Tree or an ancient oak tree. Or maybe you did and it's just something our parents and our parent's parents didn't talk about quite so openly. But whether you grew up with magical trees or not, I am willing to bet you can relate to the cloud of fear that grew throughout my adolescence.

When I began studying hypnosis, one of the first things I learned that really made me look at my personal history in a new way was the idea that children are naturally in a state of hypnosis until approximately eight years old. Now, this does not mean they are going through life in a daze or clucking like chickens. It means that they are super receptive and that they take words very literally. They believe what they're told, especially by those perceived as authority figures, i.e., adults. They have a strong connection to the spiritual side of the universe. Their creative and imaginative subconscious mind leads their life, rather than the logical and analyzing conscious mind; their cognitive abilities are not yet fully developed until about age eleven or twelve. Right smack in the center of those middle school years. This is when fear, particularly the fear of judgment, really begins to emerge.

Our conscious mind searches for ways to logically explain our experiences that our subconscious mind takes for granted. When we are unable to find logical explanations for things, like our innate connection to the spiritual world, our fear-based ego convinces us to turn away from it, to hide it, to distrust it, and to rely on what feels more comfortable instead. As herd animals, humans chose what generally seems more comfortable, which is what we see our peers doing.

So as my innate spiritual connection faded, the door was opened for my fear-based ego to quietly take over. The ego is sneaky, though, so it allowed just enough of my uniqueness to shine through that it didn't look suspicious. I began operating from a place of playing small and doing what I felt I was supposed to do to fit into the herd. I began to do more of the things that society deemed normal, and less of the things that made me, Me. I began to conform to the expectations of others rather than live from a place of authenticity and empowerment as I had always known before.

We often refer to this process as growing up or becoming a responsible adult. Enter the world of full-time employment. By the time I entered the full-time workforce, I had always held at least one job since I'd turned sixteen. When I came to the end of my undergrad career, I opted for a safe, secure, and unfulfilling job in real estate, doing administrative work and marketing. Never quite sure what I wanted to be when I "grew up," I found myself in a string of similar jobs that I quickly outgrew, always hoping one day I'd stumble upon the elusive Dream Job.

By age 35, I'd had enough and decided to go back to school to further my education in one of my first loves, theatre. I was certain that this was the ticket to a career I would feel passionate about. Finally. Two years later, with a master's degree, a mountain of debt, and being deemed overqualified for any theatre jobs I applied for, I was still working in real estate, feeling even more confused than I was before. If a career in theatre, which I absolutely love, wasn't for me... then what was?

Fear kept me playing small, so while the theatre world knew I was overqualified, they wouldn't hire me. At the same time, the real estate world recognized this and took advantage of my situation for as long as I'd be willing to stay. Mine is not a story of nightmare bosses or unbearable coworkers. I was very fortunate to have worked with some wonderful people. Instead, it was simply that I knew it wasn't the path I was meant for. Slowly, the fear that kept me playing small shifted into shame, knowing I was stuck in a cycle of mediocrity, but unable to see my path out of it.

One day, I was presented with a sparkling opportunity and a way out, Network Marketing. Full of so many promises of independence and abundance, I optimistically hoped for the best and began investing in myself and my career. While I very quickly learned that this path was not for me, it inadvertently led me to something that lit me up in an entirely new way: Hypnosis.

I was beyond intrigued. Hypnosis tied together so many of my interests, the woo-woo side of life, science, meditation, and the desire to better myself while helping others do the same. Within eight months, I was a newly certified hypnotist and began building my business on the side of my safe and secure nine-to-five job. For the first time ever, I knew I was on the right path. Business was off to an amazing start. Fear would no longer keep me in dead-end jobs. And then... March of 2020 arrived, and with it, a global pandemic. My quickly growing business screeched to a halt for the first few months, but I adapted and by August, my business was steadily making more money and bringing in more clients each month. By March 2021, I felt it was time to go all-in and decided to leave my nine-to-five to pursue hypnosis full-time.

That's when a new variety of fear set in. All the worry about failing or making the wrong choice in my decision to leave security behind began to consume me, from very the moment I gave my manager notice. As my end date approached, my fear grew steadily. It seemed as though all of my fears and worries about taking this big leap were coming true. Business slowed down. Unexpected expenses kept arising. I was terrified.

Unsure of why this was happening at the most inopportune time, I began to turn inward, focusing on my mindset. Meditating more often, journaling again, and most of all, I felt a strong call to return to nature. As I began to spend more time out in the woods and by the water, I could feel the fear calming down. I began to feel like me again. Not the "boring, safe job" me. The twelve-year-old me, who loved playing in the woods for hours on end. I felt the connection with my spiritual side that I hadn't fully entertained in years being restored. I allowed this part of me to come out again, slowly but steadily. And I began to share it more openly than I ever had before.

As my spiritual side was reawakening, I began to bring this into my hypnosis practice, both personally and with clients. Before long, my soul was pulling me in a new direction, to help others on this same journey. Because each one of us has a spiritual connection, whether we realize it or not. It is up to each of us what we choose to do with this connection.

The first step on this journey is acknowledging and releasing the fears that disconnected us from spirit in the first place. Grounding is one of my favorite tools for replacing fear with a sense of safety and security. Grounding is often used to detach your mind from overwhelm, stress, anxiety, or other distressing emotions, so it is a great tool for disarming fear when you notice it sneaking into your life. Grounding can be done in very simple ways such as spending time in nature, standing barefoot on your lawn, or taking a bath. These simple acts bring your senses back down to earth quickly.

Grounding meditation or self-hypnosis is also incredibly powerful.

Here's how to begin:

1. Sit with your spine straight and your feet planted firmly on the ground.
2. Close your eyes and tune into your breathing.
3. From the root of your spine, imagine a cord or root extending into the earth below you.
4. As you imagine the cord stretching down, also imagine it absorbing the grounding energy of the earth and filling you with a sense of safety, stability, and security.

Another great way to overcome fear is by balancing your root chakra. The root chakra is our energy field associated with safety and security. Last summer, as fear surrounding my business began to increase, I created a powerful hypnosis recording that combines grounding and root chakra balancing. It has been one of my go-to tools when I sense fear creeping in again.

You can download this recording at: www.melissaconkling.com/groundinghypnosis

One of the biggest mistakes I see people make regarding fear is labeling it as bad. Here's the thing: Fear is 100% natural and part of being human. The goal is not to exterminate fear permanently. The goal is to catch it faster, so it doesn't control your decisions and your actions.

When we make decisions from a place of fear, we allow our ego to run the show, rather than receiving guidance from our intuition and higher self. Our intuition and higher self are the direct connections with our spirit, source, the Universe, or whatever you choose to call it. They are always leading us to the course of action that is best for us to live out our soul's purpose. As we reconnect with spirit and begin to lessen our fear, we strengthen our ability to not only hear this guidance but also to trust it and to take action accordingly.

Today, while fear still shows its face regularly, I know I have the tools and the spiritual connection to lead me where I'm meant to be. I trust it wholeheartedly. It is the life-changing practice that brings me closer to my soul and my purpose each and every day.

Ewa Ladkowska

You always have a choice.

When I was growing up, I didn't know I had much choice. As a family, my parents and I traveled from Poland to Singapore to Germany. I tagged along because... well, I was a child. I was simply told, "We're moving." No matter how much I cried for my friends and my previous home, it would never be the same again.

So, there I was at age 12 in a whole new country with no German language skills whatsoever. I was told, "You need to learn German. This is the school you are going to." I had no choice in the matter. I didn't want to go to school, learn a new language, or even be in Germany. I wanted to be with my friends in Singapore, speak English, and enjoy what was familiar to me. That was my comfort zone.

After about a year or two in Germany, I was told, "Ewa, you are going to a new school on Monday." "OK. Nothing I can do about that..." I thought. So, the next day, I went to see my one and only close friend during the lunch break and told her the news. Then the next week came around, and I entered a new classroom, where I was introduced, and I obediently sat down.

I won't lie, I hated school. I was convinced no one liked me and that my German must suck because my grades weren't the best. On a school trip, I was asked once by a boy in my class if I had friends, and I thought that was a very odd thing to ask. I admitted that I did. He then asked me to name them, so I mentioned my two best friends from Singapore. Apparently, two friends, in his opinion, were not a lot. I was taken aback and decided to walk away.

When I told someone in class that they were being immature, I was told that "of course they were", because I was 2 years older than them. See... I was at least 2 years older than everyone in my class due to my German skills not being good enough after a year of learning. I was put in year 5 when I should have gone to year 7. There was no winning, I thought.

Later there was a new girl in class, who tried to get me to smile for five minutes a day. I refused to be happy. She made friends. I kept to myself.

At home, I played computer games, read books, and wrote stories. Something that I really enjoyed was acting classes which were every Friday. One of the girls in my class told me about it. These classes were separate from school. I enjoyed the people there. The girl from school that had told me about it attended a different acting group. I was put with people my age for once. We would play drama games and it was fun. Even though I felt comfortable in these sessions, I only saw these people during our 1 hour together. I didn't meet them outside of acting.

Despite acting classes, I still didn't really enjoy life. When I was 8, I was writing scripts for my toys and performing them for my parents. When I was 10, I wanted to keep on playing pretend but everyone else wanted to grow up. I was a creative child, and I was pretty sure growing up was a bad idea. When I was 15, I wanted to go to Narnia, because to me, growing up meant no fun. It meant no freedom. It meant responsibilities.

In the last two years of school, it was time to decide what I wanted to do with my life. This is when life slowly started to shift for me. I remember my mother telling me that once I finished school, I won't have to see any of my classmates ever again and I could do whatever I wanted. Then, in acting class, my teacher shared how she went to drama school and that's how she became an actor. I realized I could do it too; study acting. I thought performing was for celebrities only; that you had to be "someone's" daughter to become an actor. Now that I knew anyone could do it, I declared I was going to pursue acting.

On the last day of school, we received our certificates, and I went straight home. I didn't stay for the after-party. I was done with school and the people there. I was ready to close this chapter of my life.

That summer, I was thinking about where to go to study acting. I applied to a university to do drama and writing in the UK. I even had an online audition, passed the interview, and yet I didn't get in. They just told me I didn't get to the next stage. When I thought that I would have to stay in Germany and go with plan B, things fell into place very quickly.

Back when I had moved schools in Germany, I attended a bilingual school. Most subjects were still in German but there was an extra subject in English. The level of English taught was still too low for me, as I had learned English in Singapore. I considered myself a native speaker but at school, we were learning English as a foreign language, right from the basics. My mother thought it might be a good idea for me to have extra lessons so that I could up my level of English and so I met a wonderful lady who happened to be an English teacher. Well... technically, my mother met her in a clothing shop. After hearing her speak British, my mother approached her, and it turned out she would be the one to help me.

Rounding back to pursuing university, My English teacher moved to South Germany during my last year of school. One day during the summer, she was passing by our city, and we invited her to our house. I told her about not getting into university. She encouraged me to look up universities on the spot, find a few I liked and call them. I was nervous but I did it anyway. One university had vacancies for their drama and theatre course and after talking to them on the phone, I was told that they would love to have me. If she hadn't come that day, I wouldn't have moved to Wales.

From being the kid who hated life, I became the adult who loved life. Just like that. It's interesting to me looking back. I'm very good with people nowadays. People often tell me they love my energy, and that they feel comfortable around me. Connecting with others feels natural to me. It's like it has always been my strength even though growing up, this did not seem to be the case at all. What changed? I simply followed a new thought, "I'm going to study what I love!" This filled me with excitement. I became the biggest hugger at university and the most enthusiastic and happy person at our 9 am lectures. This was a big change for me, and everything just fell into place because I didn't resist anymore. I thought the thought until it became my reality.

Along the way, I started consuming mindset content. Life was great. Of course, I had good and bad days, but overall, life was great. One book, in particular, fell into my lap after a theatre performance. Someone had left it behind and it ended up in the lost & found box. It was called, You Can Heal Your Life by Louise Hay. When I saw that book, I knew it was meant for me.

That book taught me to love myself and that I really did have more power than I thought. I didn't realize how spiritual this book was until now. We see the world from our current perspective. I've never met Louise Hay and yet she has taught me that to heal we must feel our feelings. Change really does come from within.

Her mirror exercise was mind-blowing. In her book, she explains how she would ask her clients to look into their own eyes using a mirror while saying the statement: "I love and accept you exactly as you are." This is not an easy task. I did it a couple of years later after I had learned about Ho'oponopono, a traditional Hawaiian practice of forgiveness that involves repeating these 4 statements:

- I'm sorry.
- Please forgive me.
- Thank you.

- I love you.

This is what happened when I tried out the mirror exercise. Firstly, it took me around 15 minutes to even sit in front of the mirror without distracting myself. I kept pacing up and down the room. When I finally sat in front of the mirror, I started to see all my pimples and when I am nervous, I tend to squeeze and scratch them. After destroying my face, I started to cry but I vowed that I would finish this exercise. I looked into my eyes until I didn't see my red face anymore. It was just my eyes. I started to say the words, which was highly uncomfortable at first. I cried some more, but the more I sat there, the more I saw myself for who I was. When I used those phrases, a part of me healed. I'm sure of that. The more I looked into my own eyes, the more I saw my true self and a smile crept onto my face. I was smiling like I knew something. I just knew. Later on in my journey, I learned that the eyes are the doorway to the soul. I truly believe that, at that moment, I had seen my soul.

You'd think after reading so many self-help and mindset books, you'd be flawless. That wasn't the case. In September 2018, I moved to a new city to start my film career, and it was great. I was going outside my comfort zone, meeting new people, and learning new things. In 2019, my best friend from university moved in with me. Then 2020 came along...

It's not uncommon that 2020 brought a lot of changes; most people were deeply affected by the pandemic and had to adapt in their day-to-day lives. From lockdowns to world news, it meant adjustments had to be made. During this time, I had a massive falling out with my best friend. I didn't think I could reach such a low point in my life. My defense mechanism kicked in to protect me from experiencing conflict and pain which led me to self-isolate. I was afraid of being judged and couldn't face the world anymore. I felt like I was a bad person and that I had done something wrong. Fear took a grip on me and I hid alone inside my room, to avoid being in a room with my friend, which I knew would trigger me into a fight-or-flight mode. I disappeared off social media and barely ate. I never thought I'd ever experience an argument with someone so dear to me.

Even while experiencing what people call, "The dark night of the soul," I knew, deep down, this wasn't going to be the end of the world. I knew there were several ways to approach the situation but one thought really stuck with me, "I have to come back to myself before I take any further action." Apologising didn't feel right. I knew that I had to return to self-love first otherwise I would be taking action from a place of fear. When we make choices from fear, we create more of it. We create resistance.

With this new thought of looking within, my spiritual journey began. Although I was offline on the big social media platforms, I used my newfound time, to consume content that would lead me back to who I was. It started with numerology and listening to people speak about what was happening in the world from a spiritual perspective, which led me to explore topics of reincarnation and shadow work. I started meditating with intention and I even reconnected with a friend who I now call my soul sister. Together we shared our findings and connected with our inner guidance. Slowly, I was developing a whole new perspective on life. I started to understand that every situation was a story, an interpretation of a circumstance, and that we always had a choice.

I took up a 21-day challenge focusing on raising my vibration. This is where I really started to look at my subconscious mind and default behaviors, unearthing unconscious stories that I've been telling myself for years. I remembered information from past readings on mindset and started reapplying and practicing what I'd read about previously. When we believe we know it all, we stop growing.

While I was attending the 21-day challenge, I was staying at my parents' house in Poland. Flights had been canceled, and I had tremendous fear about returning to the UK, due to the falling out with my best friend, and I was still hiding away from most people I knew. Despite disappearing, my isolation period was much needed. It was a safe zone, and it gave me time to find my feet again.

One principle that has shaped my life, and which is the basis of what I now teach, is that everything is neutral until we give it meaning. This idea, once understood, is mind-blowing. Our world is shaped by our beliefs and thoughts which didn't even start with us. Think about it. When we are born, we don't know anything. We know how to breathe, but we don't think about it. We kept on going, never overthinking things like learning to walk.

Then slowly while growing up, we are taught how to speak and act in specific situations. We watch TV and start believing that that is how the world works. We are taught to relate to the world through comparison. I am here, you are there. It is true, we live in a world of contrast so that we can experience variety but when we overidentify with certain beliefs and thoughts, we limit ourselves and even create additional struggle.

When I realized that everything is neutral until I give it meaning, I couldn't blame or judge anything outside of myself anymore, including people. I became aware of when I was judging, and this self-awareness allowed me to let go of my struggle and take back my power. Living with my parents, for what turned out to be an entire year, gave me the chance to practice this. When I felt angry, frustrated, or upset, I reminded myself that it was nobody's fault. I even once shouted in anger that I am not blaming anyone and stormed off to my room. We are not triggered directly by what others say or do. It is what we make it mean about ourselves. If you don't particularly care about a subject, you wouldn't feel an emotional attachment to it unless you relate to it in some way.

All answers lie within. I believe we are beyond any labels that we attach to ourselves. We are meant to be who we truly are. We are here on earth to live a temporary human experience, and our soul lives on after physical death. I believe that deep down, we always know what needs to be done. Our ego will find many ways to protect us from getting hurt through procrastination and limiting beliefs about our worth. We also have a higher self, a part of ourselves that is based in pure love.

What we cannot see, we cannot change. Self-awareness is the first step to a more intentional and conscious life. This is my gift to the world. My desire is to help people become leaders by guiding them to find their own authentic path. This involves looking within and shedding the restricting labels that you have locked yourself in. An invisible cage that you are not fully aware of yet. The world really is a reflection of your inner world. The world works for you, not against you. If you are not happy with what you see around you, look at the stories you are telling yourself, because what you focus on is what you will see. When we resist the things that we do not want, they persist.

Looking back at my childhood, I was resisting moving to a new country and I created a reality where I was lonely. We cannot change the past. In fact, we cannot change the future either. What we can do is make the choices right here in the moment, now. Rather than reacting purely from the unconscious, we can respond with intention, taking aligned action. The same can be said for the falling out with my best friend. I believed I was a victim and created a reality where I lived in fear until I recognized my own story.

I've been working with my own life coach since 2017. Having someone to bring awareness to your inner narrative is very helpful. Being curious about oneself is a big gift that not everyone is willing to step into. Now that I am aware of the greatness that each of us holds, I have chosen to help others live their authentic life. What I am learning now is that we all came here to earth for a reason. We must trust the process in order to live fully. We cannot control others. We must listen to our inner guidance. This does not mean that we cannot get upset, we are here to experience emotions, and we can choose how to respond to them. Will you judge the situation or will you allow yourself to simply be you?

I am grateful for this journey even though it hurt at times. I believe there is always light in the dark. As Dumbledore from Harry Potter said, "Happiness can be found in even the darkest of times, if one only remembers to turn on the light." The universe is always watching and supporting us every step of the way.

In 2021, I discovered a new form of meditation called automatic writing. I use it to converse with the universe and channel messages to humanity. I would like to leave you with my most recent message:

"Listen to your intuition. You were born with an internal compass. You may call it your soul. Your soul came here to experience something great, to allow itself to move forward and evolve. There are indeed many options and realities in life. You do have a choice. After death, you will review these and make new choices. For now, you make decisions based on your current human experiences and perspectives. This is what needs to be focused on. The now. The past can help you understand the present but remember, there is only now. The past does not define you. You are not those labels from the past. You are fresh, every moment in time. You will never be who you were 5 minutes ago. Become the person you intend to be now. When you are, then there is no doubt you are."

– Message from the universe.

Veronica Knight

"The reason why many people feel stuck is because they place their identity in their experiences and insecurities. You are not your traumas, mistakes or past. Though the pain has been a part of your story, it should never dictate your character or chapters to come."

–Morgan Richard Olivier

You are worthy because you exist.

Think about your childhood for one minute. Was it happy? Painful? Something you do not want to think about?

Imagine weeding your garden; it's neglected and overgrown because you keep telling yourself that you will get to it tomorrow. Imagine going outside and picking up the weeds by the stems and throwing them away, thinking you were taking care of the problem. Are the weeds really gone? No. You need to go get a shovel, dig into the dirt, and pull out the roots with your bare hands. Those roots are deep! You can't expect to plant a beautiful garden of flowers if you don't have those weed roots pulled up, because they will just take over again.

This analogy explains how our subconscious works. Our environment, everything around us, influences us as soon as we are born into this world. It's filtered into the subconscious mind, which controls what we believe to be true about ourselves, and how we think and act. Everything that we have learned since we were born is deeply rooted in the subconscious and is there to keep us "safe." These beliefs AKA roots are the influences, environment, and experiences we've had that not everyone sees. The weed is what grows from those influences, and that is what we show the world through our words and actions.

One of the things I've learned on my self-healing journey is that my childhood trauma was not feeling loved and feeling unworthy. As I am working on my self-improvement journey alongside other strong supportive women, I've learned that my negative mindset came from not knowing how to show love and always asking for validation because I lacked confidence and had low self-esteem. As I continue my journey with God, I've made connections between my behaviors both past and present, through self-awareness.

As a child, I wanted to be a myriad of things, as all children do. I was laughed at or mocked because the things I shared didn't seem "reasonable." I wanted to be an actor, a model, a pilot, a teacher, or a psychologist. I grew out of the actor/model stage eventually, I think it's a pinnacle of childhood to admire the stars in our favorite movies and want to be like them. I did know that I wanted to help others, this was something that has always been true to my soul's purpose.

One of the biggest things that I remember is that I didn't feel heard. I still don't to this day by certain people, but I've learned to implement the necessary boundaries. I was the "good" child because I sought approval and did what I was told. The way others perceive me was what I believed to be important, so I acted accordingly. I became quiet. Don't get me wrong, I am naturally an introvert, I like observing, but I started to keep my feelings inside because I felt like showing emotions was bad because they were often dismissed.

I was awkward at home and school, and I was also bullied. I didn't know how to stand up for myself. To a child, this teaches them that they aren't good enough for certain things and that love was an icky thing; this belief got buried deep into my subconscious mind. I hated myself.

1985 2nd Grade

I had the most AMAZING 2nd-grade teacher. She was my favorite. I am sure you had a favorite teacher, at least I hope that you did. People that work with children are Superheroes, in my opinion. She was kind and fair, and she pushed me to do better. I struggled with subtraction, so she helped me with my math and encouraged me. She also gave me the grades that I earned, if it was subtraction, my grades sucked. Did I like it? Absolutely not! Did I appreciate it? Absolutely, because she was there for me and helped me instead of just giving me a grade that she thought I would like, just to appease me.

1988 5th Grade

I also had an amazing 5th-grade teacher. I remember being in another classroom at the beginning of the year and then being moved to hers. I don't remember why, perhaps the other teacher wasn't the right fit for me. This teacher was strict, no bullshit, and fair. As an adult, I understand now why I am drawn to people who are direct and don't bullshit. As a child, things were always sugar-coated for me to avoid hurting my feelings. She was just awesome.

1992 9th grade

If you could go back in time and tell your younger self a piece of advice, what would it be? At the end of 9th grade, I really wanted to apply to be in the IB program going forward from 10th grade. It is a program designed for 16–19-year-olds in high school. I was told, "No," several times. "It's too difficult," "You're going to have to work extra hard", etc., were phrases I heard from both my parents and a guidance counselor. So, I stopped asking and settled, but I kept thinking about it all through high school.

So, if I could go back in time, I would tell my younger self that she isn't confined to the box that she's been put into by others. She can stand up for herself when she really believes in something. She doesn't have to settle. Never, ever settle.

1995 Junior Year High School

I wanted to be in Junior Miss in high school. It was a fun pageant for the female students to show off their talents. It was very similar to a talent show. I wanted to participate because I thought it would be fun, period. When I asked if I could have permission to participate, I was met with resistance. I was told, "You're going to be competing against girls who have been dancing since they were three!" and "There's a lot of competition out there!" I stood my ground, participated, and had one of the best experiences in high school.

College 1996-2003

My standards were pretty low for myself. I'd always had a protective bubble around me and then I escaped to college. I was in this nice, neat little box that others put me in until I moved away from home and then I don't know what the hell happened.

I joined a fantastic sorority during the Spring of my freshman year of college. It was an awesome time of bonding with other women whose goals were in alignment with my own at the time: to support one another as we journeyed through college and graduated, to see us off into the world. I felt like I was a part of something, and that I belonged. Do you know that feeling? I hope you do. I hope you still have that feeling for something that you are doing as you are reading this. If you don't, then I hope I can be part of your inspiration as you read through this.

I didn't know what I wanted to do with my life. I spent a lot of all-nighters staring at my computer screen hoping the answer would just jump out of the computer screen at me. I started to have family drama back home and I started to just not care about the classes. I went out with my sorority sisters because it made me feel better. I wasn't doing my homework, I went to a lot of sorority parties, had too much to drink, and slept in when I should have been going to class; drowning my sorrows in alcohol and partying. Trying to make friends, I did not know how to communicate well, as I had always considered myself socially awkward.

Spring 1998 – Sophomore Year, CSU

Failure is a great lesson. It's a teaching tool. Saying, "Failure isn't an option!" is a bunch of BS. Who says that!? You need to fail to grow, otherwise, you will be stuck in the same pile of crap… and who wants that? Unless you like sitting in a pile of stink. What do I know? To each his own. With that being said, by the end of my Sophomore year in college, I flunked out of the four-year university I had worked hard to get into.

Fall 1999 – Junior Year, City College

I crawled. I had to crawl my way back into the University. I was an embarrassment to myself. I enrolled in the city college, which was an awesome place. I just loved school, so I didn't really care where I was, as long as I got back in at a school. While I took courses that put me on the path to my teaching career, I also went back to the University to talk to professors, in hopes of getting some of those "Fs" off my record. I pleaded insanity to those professors. I had to write them letters telling them why I failed their classes, in hopes they would give me grace.

I told them that I was having family problems back home, that I was depressed, and couldn't handle it. My dad was diagnosed with Stage 4 cancer at that time. I wanted him to see me graduate from college. I told them that my goal was to be a teacher and I just wanted a reprieve. Some professors were compassionate and gave me "I's", which is considered incomplete but counted. Some were not very understanding and just told me to suck it up and make the classes back up. So, I put on my Big Girl panties and got serious. I am now in my 18th year teaching.

2011

I stopped drinking in 2011. It wasn't doing me any favors. I realized that I was breaking my own heart and I was using alcohol to drown out the feelings I wanted to avoid. The last straw was when a very good friend of mine blocked me after we got into an argument in an exchange of put-downs and insults. I was arguing with him over social media while I was drinking. This is significant because I had allowed this person to use me for a few years while I was in college and I had a boyfriend at that time, back in 1999.

My gut had screamed at me to not engage in the behaviors I was engaging in with him. But wanting to feel loved and accepted over caring about my self-worth took over. I just wanted a friend, but he took advantage of our friendship. And because of that, I became emotionally attached to his behaviors and how he treated women in his life, which was shitty. During our drunken argument, I was trying to tell him what to do and how to live his life. I had no business doing that, even though I thought I was being a good friend. I wasn't.

2022

God is my CONSTANT RECHARGE. He is my reminder that I can be who I really am by fixing my focus on HIM. For that, I am grateful.

In the grand scheme of things, it was only a few years ago that I felt lost. Back then I felt like when I reached out to others, I was grasping for air, and I couldn't breathe. I was in a local women's Facebook support group I made a few posts in, hoping to connect, but it never happened.

I no longer feel the need to vent to anyone. I cast those onto Him, let Him carry my burdens. These were two posts that I had made"

July 22, 2020:

I need some support. I don't have any close friends or know whom I can talk to. Just being honest.

November 12, 2020:

In my feelings today. Had a trigger dream that happens about once a month. No, I don't want to talk about it. But I'm sure many can relate. It sucks.

December 2020:

I ended up in the hospital with one of the worst flares of my life, hardly able to move. I had been teaching remotely, so I wasn't sharing germs... I really believe stress was the trigger. I had to do something.

March 16, 2021:

I had a dream, God slammed the door in my face. My trigger dream no longer existed after this point. Have you ever woken up gasping for air, feeling like you've been punched in the gut?

May 2021 - Spiritual Awakening:

I gave in to God, started to Listen and I haven't looked back... I was so tired and fed up with my circumstances and feeling stuck. I knew that there was something bigger for me, and I was going to be damned if I didn't go for it, even if it meant stepping out of my comfort zone that I had been in for about 35 years.

I just want you to know that whatever it is that you are going through, Just be. And it will be OK. I promise. On the other side of the struggle sometimes you will be SO grateful to God for everything, even the things that felt painful to live through, that it will make you cry.

2022 - A Spiritual Breakthrough:

Using intuitive writing, I had my conversation with God:

Dear God,

Help me understand why I have this desire to hear or see nice words being said to me.

G: Why are you asking?

Because when I see words of affirmation, it makes me feel good and I believe them when they are used consistently.

G: So, when you write your affirmations in the morning to yourself, doesn't it make you feel good?

Yes.

G: Do you believe them?

Yes, because I go and put action behind the affirmations that I tell myself... I am consistent.

G: So, what's your question about other people?

I think I'm sorting out my thoughts here... I grew up with people calling me names or belittling me. I recall a few times hearing someone close to me say something, or hearing other people that were supposed to be nice, but it just sounds fake.

G: Why did it sound fake?

Because they were not things that typically came out of this person’s mouth. It was more like it's in the moment, "let me say this so I look good," kind of thing. It was not consistent behavior. So, it was fake to me.

G: Back to your original question... is it the same or is it a different question you are trying to ask about?

I think I am having a hard time accepting people I know, who genuinely mean their words of affirmation because they are consistent... but the rare times they don't include one... I guess it’s because I'm so used to it, it bothers me.

G: Why does it bother you?

Inconsistencies bother me.

G: Are you perfect?

No.

G: Have they done anything else different?

Not really.

G: Do you think... you are projecting your own trust issues onto them?

Could be.

G: Let's talk about reactions for a minute. What is a reaction?
A reaction is something done on impulse, no reasonable thought has been given.

G: What is a response?

A response is something done with reasonable thought.

G: Now let's circle back to your thoughts when you see someone say something to you without that affirmation. What goes through your mind when you see it?

It's an immediate reaction (thought) in my head.

G: So, you impulsively automatically assume they don't like you, love you, or value you because they didn't say a word you wanted to hear?

Yes.

G: Is that reasonable?

No.

G: Can you tell me something else you've learned about reacting?
Yes. "My reaction to you is an awareness of me."

G: So, what does that mean in your situation?

It looks like I am projecting my own insecurities onto someone else. I need to get over myself.

G: What can you do so that you preserve your relationships and not harm them just because you have those past trauma issues?

Be the person I needed when I was younger. Continue using affirmations to them consistently like I have been and stop questioning their motives when they don't say something I want to hear. Otherwise, it becomes an if/then situation that I was brought up in. Break the cycle or I will just continue it.

November 2022 The Power of the Pause

There is a fine balance between doing and being. I've spent a lot of 2022 working on being still, pausing to self-reflect, and being in the moment. I have taken at least three personal ME days off this school year so that I could rest and work on things that were getting neglected.

Sometimes we get so caught up in trying to meet the goals that we have made for ourselves that we forget that we need to give ourselves grace, patience, time, and love along the way... we are human after all. Aim for progress, not perfection, and quality over quantity. If you only focus on the destination, you will miss the moments that count. The joy is in the journey.

One of the biggest lessons that I have learned so far, and that I am continuing to learn, is to LISTEN to the voice that whispers, "Wait." When you hear that voice say "Wait," listen to it. Self-control is a big challenge for many. The only way you can master it is when you are still. Be still. Emotions are temporary, so don't let them overpower your intelligence and intuition. Ego will rule your emotions if you let it. Shift your mindset. Game changer.

Speak less, listen more. React less, observe more. Some of you might not want to hear this, but the best way to practice this is by being still and pausing, this is when you have some time to yourself. Learn to like yourself, and once you master that, love yourself.

You are worthy. I love you. I am proud of you.

Amanda Rose

Master Your Mind and You Master Your Life.

To be spiritually awakened simply means remembering the true origins and aspects of self. It's deconstructing the layers of beliefs, identity, and ego, that we've attained during our human experience. Under it all... you're pure energy. Infinite and eternal. The creator and the created. You're a soul, temporarily in a body with a mind; not a body with a mind and a soul.

I grew up in a very spiritual household, which I didn't realize until I got into public school was not normal. As a young child, I practiced meditation, played with crystals and essential oils, reveled in understanding myself better through astrology, and drew tarot cards at each moon phase. My mother's bookshelf was full of books on divination, tarot, astrology, spirituality, the law of attraction, and a slew of other kinds of self-help and spiritual endeavors. Looking back, as an adult, I'm extremely grateful for this early exposure. Children have this beautiful connection to the non-physical plane of existence and can be incredible messengers for ideas from Universe Consciousness to channel through.

For as long as I can remember, I've known my life's purpose. I incarnated in this human form to be a guide, to help humanity shift their way of thinking, break free of old outdated cycles, and step into their true infinite power. It's always been my destiny to help people move towards living intentional lives, tapping into abundance, chasing their dreams, and feeling fulfilled. When I was a child, I assumed I'd do this through the arts, with film and music.

As I got older, I got more entrenched in the daily to-dos of life. My spiritual practices waned, and my attention drifted to scholastic studies, and eventually, work. I was wrapped up in the happenings of the physical world. Of course, it's not as if I forgot all I'd grown up learning and experiencing, it simply wasn't a priority at that stage of my life.

As an adolescent, I began to struggle with a deep heavy depression. Life felt flat. I fantasized about suicide but had no intention of following through; I knew enough spiritually to know that if I killed myself, I'd just reincarnate, and would need to go through it all over again. It made more sense to persevere.

I was obese growing up. By age 15 I was 258 pounds and miserable. Unbeknownst to me, until years later, childhood trauma had led me to have a binge eating disorder from a very young age. I had a burning inner desire to be a famous actress, and... everyone on screen was skinny! So, I committed once and for all to lose weight. Within a month my "diet" snowballed into full-blown anorexia.

For a year and four months, I only ate 1/3 of a measuring cup of food 3 times a day. I also exercised intensely for 60 minutes every day. My body went through hell. The only saving grace was that thankfully, I took a big handful of vitamins every day to make up for the nutrients I wasn't getting through food.

During that horrendous time, I had no energy, my periods stopped (and didn't return for about 5 years), my hair fell out, I cried randomly, and as the weight came off, you could count my ribs; even sleeping hurt my body. I weighed myself 20+ times a day. I developed some obsessive-compulsive tendencies. I had body dysmorphia. I retreated from my friends. The worst part though? The torturous self-bullying between my ears. It took years and years of therapy and healing to finally move through this mental illness. Eventually, in my late 20's, diving deeply into mindset practices, I finally learned to love myself again.

I graduated from the Acting for Film and TV Program at Humber College, in 2008, and took a 1-year creative writing program at the college after. Graduating into the recession, I found that I couldn't land a job for about a year, despite being an honor roll student with A grades, and the Governor General's award to boot. When I finally got work, it was door-to-door sales, certainly not what I'd hoped for. The next few years had me bouncing from job to job, retail, then live-instore sales presentations, until finally... I'd had enough.

I quit, without a plan, and just a few months of savings to live on. I didn't want to work for anyone else anymore, and I wanted to get back on track with my life's purpose. Without knowing what else to do, I ended up joining a network marketing company.

The years that followed me challenged me in a multitude of ways. I struggled to get my online business profitable. The first year I made a measly $600. Living under the poverty line was challenging. Ironically, people think that all rich people do is think about money, when in reality, it's when you don't have enough money that you cannot stop thinking about it.

During this time, the Universe was trying to give me hints, subtly, about what I needed to do to get out of the struggle, but I ignored them. People kept talking about reading personal development books, but I'd always say, "I know that stuff already," dismiss it, and focus back on strategy. The truth is, there's a huge difference between knowing of something, and knowing about something because you live it day-in and day-out.

The Universe kept trying to give me this message, and I continuously ignored it, until... I couldn't anymore. Near the end of 2016, my husband came home one day and handed me a letter without saying a word. I was dubious at this strange behavior from him. I promptly opened it to see that he'd been fired from his job. Immediately my mind raced, and my heart sped up; by that point, I was only earning roughly $600-1000 a month, certainly not enough to live on. I was worried we'd lose our car, our house, and... everything.

As the panic began to settle, I saw two very clear paths in front of me that I needed to choose from. The first path was learning how to file for bankruptcy. The second path was getting over my ego and diving once-and-for-all into my money bullshit and healing it. I chose the second path.

With a focus on saving every penny we had, I opted for books to be my teachers during this time. I got my hands on all the books I could on money, mindset, and manifesting. I not only read them, but I applied what I learned, which is more challenging than it sounds. Many of the practices forced me to do some extremely uncomfortable deep dives into my belief system and my old money wounds. However, as the saying goes, "The only way out is through."

While it didn't seem like it at the time, there is no better time to change than when you are facing weighty consequences for not changing. My situation felt dire, there were very real possibilities of losing everything, and as you can imagine, that made it very difficult to stay positive and redirect my thoughts toward what I was building, rather than what I was hoping to avoid.

The brain is programmed to watch out for danger. We call it the "survival mind," and it's that voice in your head that is always pointing out what's wrong, what could go wrong, and why it's too scary, risky, etc. to pursue the things you desire. It takes a lot of practice to learn to gently, and lovingly, redirect our thoughts toward what it is we desire.

Interestingly, when you go white water rafting, instructors will tell you, "I will only point in the direction I want you to row towards, I will never point at the jagged rocks, or a downed tree that we should avoid, because if I do, you'll unconsciously start rowing towards it." You've probably heard the saying, "What you focus on expands." Whatever you think about becomes your reality, so it's key we learn to think about what we desire VS what we do not.

The mind is fascinating. In any given second, your subconscious mind is aware of approximately 4 billion bits of information, while by contrast, your conscious mind is aware of only about 2000 bits. This begs the question, out of 4,000,000,000 bits of information available, how does the conscious mind pick which 2,000 to be aware of? The answer is: the ones you tell it to. Your focus dictates your awareness.

Have you ever noticed, when you get a new car, new shoes, or a new book, you start to see people with that same object all over the place? Once it came into your awareness, your mind picked up on it all over. It wasn't that suddenly everyone else went out and got that thing too, they already had it, you just weren't aware of it.

As I began to understand my mind, and how my beliefs were governing my outcomes, I peeled back the layers to uncover the lessons I needed to learn. I came to realize, that underneath it all, I had some very unhelpful money beliefs that were keeping me broke.

While I was doing all this inner work, I started to notice subtle changes almost immediately. I was surprised, because, I really hadn't changed anything I'd been doing strategically. Suddenly, people were proactively reaching out to me and asking how they could work with me.

It was an emotionally strenuous 6 months following my husband's layoff, however, at the end of that time we'd manifested over 6-figures and it was utterly life-changing. We ended up moving into a beautiful new home in a different city. I had a burning desire to share what I'd learned; the Law of Attraction radically changed my life so fast, I wanted to scream it from the rooftops!

I created my first Manifesting online program, The Law of Attraction 3-week Retreat, and I rekindled my old dream of being an author. I pulled out the first manuscript I'd ever written, Fire Fury Freedom, back from when I was 16, and started editing it. I also began interviewing authors and studying book marketing and the various publication methodologies available. It become very clear that self-publishing was the best option. I spoke to over 100 authors, and none of them recommended small or medium publishing companies; no one had a good experience with one. Then the gigantic publishers only accepted manuscripts through literary agents, and that was a long arduous process to pursue on a "maybe one day someone will pick it up," hope. Self-publishing offered control, distribution, a full share of the royalties, and was also non-exclusive, so I could sign with a publisher should a great fit arise.

As the editing process was wrapping up, I decided to do a test run with self-publishing. So, I turned my 3-week law of attraction course into a book, Manifesting on Purpose, which ironically, is my best-selling book to date. Nothing is coincidental.

Since then, I've gone on to publish over 20 books, develop over 40 life-changing programs, do a slew of TV, magazine, podcast, and blog interviews, and be a guest speaker at innumerable summits. In the Spring of 2019, I got to be a guest author at the Toronto Comicon convention with my science fiction series, the Fire Fury Saga. In September 2019, I founded my corporation, The Infinite Power of You Inc. In 2020 I started the No BS Biz Show podcast with an old high school friend, and fellow entrepreneur, Tony Babcock. In July of 2021 we co-founded The No BS Biz Co. Ltd., and that same month, my husband and I moved into our dream house, a stunning mini-mansion in the countryside amidst the Canadian Shield. In 2022 I officially become a self-made millionaire. I share all of this so you can see how radically fast your life can change; within 5 years I went from under the poverty line to a self-made millionaire. If I can, so can you.

Ultimately, our 3-dimensional problems are our best teachers for spiritual growth and expanding our consciousness. While they may test us, cajole us, and upset us in the midst of living through them, once we learn to let go of our egoic need to control the situations we face, and instead, seek out the lesson in them, we grow, and the solutions present themselves. Life is the best teacher we have.

Whatever challenges you've faced, no matter how grueling, have been for the spiritual evolution of your soul. The lessons you learned from those experiences are invaluable. I believe those lessons are why we're here and intrinsically linked to our soul purpose. Whatever you have overcome, you can help others overcome; it's a beautiful way of paying it forward with love.

Meet The Authors

Taylor LaShay

Taylor Lashay is a Holistic Leadership Coach, Energy healer, and the CEO of Insight to the Inside Coaching. She empowers leaders of self and soul to claim healthy soul-aligned relationships without people pleasing by raising their soul standards for their life vision through self-dependability. It's her passion to help self-leaders from all walks of life to live more empowered on a soul level, so that they can be, do, and have a reality that matches their soul goals. Taylor believes no goal is unattainable and empowers the people that come into her energy to be themselves unapologetically while reaching for their dreams that some people say are crazy to have.

Taylor's years of leadership allow her to give more unique support to her clients. She helps people gain insight to the inside of how to better lead themselves and create more aligned solutions spiritually and holistically, by deepening the relationships they have with their mind, body, soul, and surroundings. Her personal journey of generational healing, self-healing, and soul expansion, also allows her to really help her clients go beyond just getting by and overcome self-sabotaging thoughts and feelings through self and soul empowerment.

Visit: https://taylor-lashay.mykajabi.com/

Crystal Wheeler

Crystal Wheeler was born in the quiet mountains of Tennessee. She Moved to Alabama at the age of 3 where she was raised in a very conservative area of town. She has overcome many obstacles in life from having an abusive childhood and battling an eating disorder to leaving a strict religious community.

She strives to instill self-love and positivity into everyone she encounters. She broke through many barriers that were meant to destroy her. But she is still standing strong today. At 33 years old she lives in Florida. She is the owner of a leggings company LegsForDaze. Her life's mission is to heal other people through helping them to learn self-confidence and self-care.

Visit: etsy.com/shop/LegsforDazee

Alea Marie Quiles

Alea Marie Quiles is the Founder and CEO of Becoming Clutterless, LLC. She is a Professional Organizer and Declutterer of mind and home, Reiki Master Teacher, Feng Shui enthusiast, Certified Breathe Coach, and Published Author of Multiple Works, including Activating Your Inner Alchemist. Alea specializes in helping her clients clear the chaos so they can fill their hearts and home with harmony and unlock their unlimited potential through intuitive practices and effective strategies.

Connect with Alea:

www.facebook.com/thisisaleamarie

www.pinterest.com/BecomingClutterless

Kirsten Newman

Kirsten Newman (aka The Soul Doula) is a spiritual coach, author, course creator, and channel of the divine feminine. She specializes in serving others who are ready to reconnect with and surrender to their own divine feminine essence and activate the unfolding of their purpose, medicine, leadership, and manifestation.

As a healer as well as a coach, Kirsten believes the work of creating your desires and living the life you truly adore is a sacred journey of healing, activation, and alignment. She brings this belief into the loving space she holds for her clients at all times, and this shines brightly through her clients' quantum transformations.

Blending energy healing, shadow work, somatic experiencing, past life regressions, light language activations, astrology, human design, gene keys, mindset, and embodiment work, Kirsten firmly believes that every single person drawn to her work is here to step up into their own potent divine feminine leadership and birth their medicine through it into the world. She believes our bodies hold the codes and wisdom to unlock this blueprint.

Kirsten has been coaching and healing since 2017 and stands proudly and passionately in her soul mission to help as many others as possible to share their medicine and magic in support of the raising of the collective's vibration as we move ever closer to New Earth.

You can follow her work here:

www.instagram.com/the_soul_doula

Allison Barnett

Allison Barnett is the CEO and Founder of BRG Unlimited LLC., a premier Luxury Real Estate Agent, Channeler, Energy Shifter, and Manifestation & Business Coach. Her practice is rooted in spirituality, offering a unique blend of energetic mastery and industry experience to create magic with her clients.

Taking an unconventional approach to business that includes intuitive guidance and manifestation techniques, Allison built her career upon the foundation of a Juris Doctorate cum Laude from John Marshall Law School and a Bachelor of Science in

Communications and Broadcasting from the University of Tennessee. She then carved a niche for herself as an Intuitive Realtor experienced in the areas of new construction, sales management, design, luxury, coaching, and more.

Allison appeared on The Negotiators, a Reveel Entertainment original series, for her I-Buyer knowledge. She was also featured in Top Agent Magazine and The Mortgage Reports, as well as guest appearances on various podcasts. Allison has received numerous awards and recognitions, including an appointment to the launch team for Hoodle, being named Best of Woodstock, and continued membership in the MultiMillion Dollar Club.

Focused on helping clients navigate their next moves, personally and professionally, Allison continues to practice real estate, while mentoring agents and business owners to manifest and uplevel, locally and abroad. In addition, she produces her own YouTube channel, The Allison Barnett Show, co-creates for the Craig and Alli brand, and collaborates with her husband, Knox, on joint business ventures.

Visit AllisonBarnett.live for offers and opportunities to make magic happen with Allison.

Sarah Lines

Sarah Lines helps soul-driven, spiritual entrepreneurs on a mission to delete their old paradigms to more deeply connect with their inner being and activate their purpose. As a Soul-Life-Biz Alchemist and channel, Sarah leads visionary women into superconscious creation to manifest the life and business of their dreams, catapulting them into a new energy of radiance, abundance, and purpose-driven lives.

With lifetimes of experience, she has helped hundreds of clients awaken, ascend & powerfully create new realities. Creator of the Goddess Alchemy Academy, Sarah has authored multiple books including international best sellers.

Lyndy Perez

Lyndy Perez considers herself a doula for the living and the dying. She is the owner of The Blue Lotus Path. Traditionally, a doula is someone who is employed to provide guidance and support to a pregnant woman during labor. Lyndy is happily enjoying her path and calling as a guide and mentor for those that desire to change the course trajectory or pattern of their Life (Life Doula). Lyndy also assists those transitioning from Life to Death (Death Doula), as well as assisting their loved ones during the painful and difficult time of preparing for the death of their loved one. She is also a meditation guide and energy worker - helping those beings realign holistically - mind, body, and spirit.

Melissa Conkling

Melissa Conkling is a Certified Professional Hypnotist, NLP Practitioner, and Life Coach based in Connecticut and working with clients virtually around the world. Driven by her own spiritual awakening and personal transformation, she focuses on helping spiritually minded people reprogram their subconscious minds for inner empowerment and authentic living without endless surface-level work using transformational hypnosis and coaching.

As a lover of nature, she feels most connected to spirit while walking through the woods or relaxing by the ocean, where her spiritual journey began and where her re-awakening started and continues to grow each day.

She was named one of the 10 Best Hypnotists by Natural Nutmeg magazine in 2020, 2021, and 2022 and has been featured on many podcasts, including the Work Smart Hypnosis podcast and A Guided Life Podcast.

Visit: https://www.melissaconkling.com/

Grab Melisa's Grounding Hypnosis Here:

https://www.melissaconkling.com/groundinghypnosis

Jaime Zazzara

Jaime Zazzara has 22 years of experience as an educator. It has always been her mission to empower and instill a positive-growth mindset in everyone she meets. She found her purpose after experiencing a challenging divorce and healing after being codependent and married to an alcoholic.

Jaime is a Professional Life Coach specializing in wellness, spirituality, and mindset. She assists women in letting go of the past and learning to love themselves while living a balanced, happy life. Jaime's goal is to spread love and light through empowerment, speaking, writing, and coaching while connecting with and inspiring others.

Jaime hosts Wind Therapy Wellness Retreat sails in the summer on the Jersey Shore. This includes a 3-hour sail along the bay with guided meditation, mindfulness, yoga, and singing bowls. She serves as a Spiritual Mindset Coach and Social Emotional Learning Consultant.

Jaime is the creator of Teach P.E.A.C.E, a Social Emotional Learning program for children. She is trained as an advanced facilitator by The Center for Mind Body Medicine. Jaime is a motivational Speaker and Author. Her books titled, "Freedom in Forgiveness" and "Let It Go Let It Flow" can be found on Amazon. Her online courses include Let it Go, and Let it Flow, and 28 Day Meditation Challenge. Her in-person events include: Full Moon Chakra Bowl Meditation, New Moon Women's Circle, Vision Board Workshop, Chakra Healing Course, Cord Cutting Ceremony, and Forgiveness Labyrinth.

Connect with Jaime Zazzara, JZ Heals, LLC
Website: https://linktr.ee/jaimezazzara
Facebook:

Biz FB: www.facebook.com/jzheals

www.facebook.com/windtherapywellness

Instagram: www.instagram.com/jzheals/

Email: jaimezazzara@gmail.com

Ewa Ladkowska

Ewa Ladkowska is the Founder of Myrrh Song Coaching. (Myrrh being her soul's name rediscovered through a guided meditation) She is a life and spiritual coach calling herself the creative guide. It is important for her to highlight that her work provides guidance rather than giving advice. Because of her background in performance, she is focusing on helping blocked creatives unearth their next creative masterpiece.

Ewa specializes in assisting her clients in developing self-awareness, opening the ability to transform current thoughts into ones that create more love, happiness & peace. This will allow clients to uncover their endless source of creativity and progress in their passion projects. Ewa is currently offering free deep dives and 1:1 coaching.

Alongside coaching, Ewa is an actor, model, podcast host on Guided 888, and intuitive guide where she channels through writing and sharing the results online.

Instagram: @myrrhsong

Veronica Knight

Veronica Knight is a life and mindset coach for moms, committed to empowering moms to transform self-limiting beliefs to create a life of confidence and clarity.

Connect with Veronica:

https://www.linkedin.com/in/VeronicaKnight1204/

Amanda Rose

Amanda Rose is the CEO and founder of The Infinite Power of You INC., Co-Founder of No BS Biz Co. Ltd., a Business, Wealth and Mindset Coach, Multi-Published Multi-Genre Bestselling Author, Motivational Speaker, Course Creator, Actor, and

Self-Made Millionaire. Her corporation serves entrepreneurs worldwide, with her unique approach that focuses on understanding each client's individual strengths and guiding them in building their own methodology, rather than attempting to get them to adapt to a specific mold.

Amanda has been a sales expert for over a decade, having experience in door-to-door sales, retail, live sales presentation, network marketing, and online product and service sales, which allows her to bring extensive insight to her clients. Amanda has been featured in many publications and news articles for her work, including FOX, CBS, Yahoo! Finance, and NBC, and was recently recognized with the BRAINZ Global 500 Award and the CREA 2021 Award. Amanda passionately works to help entrepreneurs succeed through her Corporation as well as within her Facebook Community.

Visit: https://amanda-rose.mykajabi.com/

Made in the USA
Monee, IL
28 April 2023

32617402R00102